AQA History B

International Relations: Conflict and Peace in the 20th Century

GCSE

Jim McCabe
David Ferriby
Tony Hewitt
Alan Mendum

Nelson Thornes

Published in 2009 by:
Nelson Thornes Ltd
Delta Place
27 Bath Road
CHELTENHAM
GL53 7TH
United Kingdom

13 14 15 16 / 10 9 8 7 6 5

A catalogue record for this book is available from the British Library

978 1 4085 0301 0

Illustrations by: Dave Russell

Page make-up by Fakenham Photosetting, Norfolk

Printed in China

Contents

Nelson Thornes

Nelson Thornes has worked hard to ensure this book and the accompanying online resources offer you excellent support for your GCSE course.

You can feel assured that they match the specification for this subject and provide you with useful support for this course.

These print and online resources together **unlock blended learning**; this means that the links between the activities in the book and the activities online blend together to maximise your understanding of a topic and help you achieve your potential.

These online resources are available on which can be accessed via the internet at **www.kerboodle.com/live**, anytime, anywhere. If your school or college subscribes to *kerboodle* you will be provided with your own personal login details. Once logged in, access your course and locate the required activity.

For more information and help on how to use *kerboodle* visit **www.kerboodle.com**.

How to use this book

Objectives

Look for the list of **Learning Objectives** based on the requirements of this course so you can ensure you are covering what you need to know.

Study tip

Don't forget to read the **Study tips** throughout the book as well as answering **Practice Questions**.

Visit **www.nelsonthornes.com** for more information.

GCSE History B

■ Unit 1: International Relations: Conflict and Peace in the 20th Century

This book covers *AQA GCSE History Specification B Unit 1: International Relations: Conflict and Peace in the 20th Century*. As an outline study, the Specification does not cover all the events of the 20th Century but concentrates on two broad themes: the causes of war and attempts to prevent the further outbreak of wars. It covers the causes of the two World Wars, the Cold War and the Crises of the Cold War and the attempts to solve these disputes. The AQA Specification is divided into six parts each of which has two key questions which are referred to as key issues. Each key issue is explained in a series of bullet points which indicate the historical knowledge needed for the study.

You will notice that this book has six chapters, each one corresponding to one part of the specification. The title of each chapter is the same as the heading given for each part in the AQA Specification. Each chapter then has two subtitles which are the key issues named in the specification.

In the GCSE examination for Unit 1, there are six questions – one on each of the six chapters in the book. You must answer any three questions.

This book guides you through the history of the period and also has a series of tasks and activities which are designed to help you to check your understanding of the issues and give you practice in evaluating a variety of sources. Throughout the text there are study tips which will guide you. At the end of each chapter you are given an example of a practice question and the mark allocation.

1.1 Why were there two armed camps in Europe in 1914?

Objectives

In this chapter you will learn about:

the Great Powers that existed at the beginning of the 20th century

the nature of the alliances that were formed between the Great Powers

the crises that affected these alliances

the build-up of armies, navies and weapons

how an assassination caused a world war.

A *The assassination of Archduke Franz Ferdinand*

The First World War broke out in 1914. The root causes lay in the alliance systems that were formed in Europe and in the crises that arose in Morocco and the Balkans. The rivalry between the alliances led countries to increase their armed forces and to develop war plans. It was the tensions caused by these alliances and crises that resulted in the assassination of Archduke Franz Ferdinand which triggered off the war plans and lead to the start of the First World War.

The Triple Alliance

This alliance between Germany, Austria-Hungary and Italy was signed in 1882. It was organised by Bismarck, the Chancellor of Germany. Germany had defeated France in the Franco-Prussian War of 1870–71, and taken the provinces of Alsace and Lorraine from the French. This victory led to the unification of German states as one country, Germany, with the King of Prussia becoming *Kaiser* (Emperor). Bismarck realised that France would want revenge, so he made a series of alliances that isolated France. The Triple Alliance formed a central block of countries across Europe, separating France from Russia. It was a defensive alliance and all three powers promised to fight if they were attacked by any other two powers.

Tasks

1   Why did Bismarck try to prevent France from gaining allies?

2   What was the importance of the Franco-Russian Alliance for:
   a   France;
   b   Europe?

3   Do you agree with the views expressed in Source **C**?

Hint

When answering Task 3, consider which parts of Source **C** you agree with and which you disagree with, explaining why and using your own knowledge to support your view.

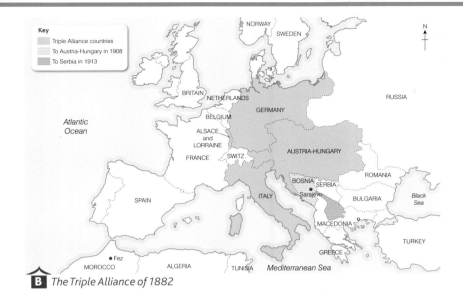

Key
- Triple Alliance countries
- To Austria-Hungary in 1908
- To Serbia in 1913

B *The Triple Alliance of 1882*

The Franco-Russian Alliance

After its defeat by Prussia in 1870, France was forced to sign the Treaty of Frankfurt in 1871, in which it lost the provinces of Alsace and Lorraine to Germany and was forced to pay Germany a sum of 5 billion francs (£200 million) in war debts. The French hatred of Germany and their wish for revenge dominated their foreign policy in the years leading up to the First World War. However, they could not get revenge on their own. After Bismarck was dismissed by Kaiser Wilhelm II in 1890, France was able to sign an agreement with Russia in 1893.

> *The Emperor of Germany has received a blow which he will bitterly resent. There is no doubt that the formal alliance of France and Russia makes it impossible for him to be the controller of Europe which he hopes to become. The Franco-Russian Alliance is at least as powerful as the Triple Alliance.*

C *From* The New York Times, *29 August 1897*

This was a strange alliance between the **autocratic Tsar** of Russia and the people's **republic** of France. The Tsar would have preferred to ally with Germany, but the Kaiser was not interested. The fact that talks between Russia and France lasted for two years before an agreement was eventually signed in 1893 shows that they were reluctant allies. The alliance became much firmer when the French loaned money to the Russians for the development of railway projects.

The terms of the alliance were defensive. Both powers agreed to join the other in war if either of them was attacked by Germany or Austria-Hungary. This alliance was a great success for France. It had emerged from isolation. Europe was divided into two armed camps and, in the event of a war, Germany was likely to have to face an attack on its western frontier from France and in the east from Russia. This meant that Germany would have to divide its forces if war broke out.

Timeline

The build-up to the First World War

1882	Triple Alliance
1893	Franco-Russian Alliance
1898	First German Naval Law
1900	Second German Naval Law
1902	Anglo-Japanese Alliance
1904	Entente Cordiale
1905	First Moroccan Crisis
1906	Algeçiras Conference
	Britain launches first Dreadnought
1907	Anglo-Russian Agreement
1908	Bosnian Crisis
1911	Agadir Crisis (Second Moroccan Crisis)
1912	First Balkan War
1913	Second Balkan War
1914	Assassination of Archduke Franz Ferdinand at Sarajevo

Key terms

Alliance: an agreement between two or more countries to support each other.

Autocratic: having complete power.

Tsar: the emperor of Russia; also spelt Czar.

Republic: a government chosen by the people with an elected president.

Study tip

You will not get a question on the details of the formation of the Franco-Russian Alliance because it took place before 1900, but it is important to understand the background behind later events.

Britain and splendid isolation

At the end of the 19th century, Britain played little part in events in Europe. It was quite happy to remain isolated from any of the alliances in Europe as long as no single power gained complete control. This isolation, because it was a deliberate policy on the part of Britain, became known as 'splendid isolation'. It depended on the strength of the British navy. Britain was an island and needed a strong navy for protection and to keep open trade and communications with its empire, which was the largest in the world.

Most of Britain's problems had involved clashes with France and Russia in the colonies. Britain began to realise that the Franco-Russian Alliance could be directed against it. Britain's natural ally was Germany: it was not a colonial power and was not therefore seen as a rival to Britain. Moreover, the royal families of the two countries were related. One of the themes of the years 1900 to 1914 is how Germany, from being Britain's most likely ally, became its enemy in the First World War.

> 66 *When Queen Victoria died in 1901, she left to her son Edward VII the richest and most powerful empire in the world, and the Royal Navy guaranteed its security. Although challenges to British supremacy came from many sides, splendid isolation still seemed possible in the new century.* 99

D From Uneasy Splendour by A. J. P. Taylor, 1968

Two events between 1898 and 1902 made Britain question its policy of splendid isolation. In 1898 Germany began to build a navy. Britain could not understand this as Germany had no empire and had the strongest army in Europe. Many in Britain thought that it was to challenge Britain's supremacy at sea. In 1899 the Boers in South Africa rebelled against Britain. Britain became involved in the Boer War, which lasted until 1902. Most of Europe sympathised with the Boers and the Kaiser made his views on this public, which further annoyed Britain.

Did you know ??????

The **Boers** were Dutch farmers who had settled in South Africa and were fighting to keep their independence from Britain.

Activities

1 Find a map that shows the extent of the British Empire in 1900.

a Which continents did it stretch to?

b Which countries could challenge Britain in these areas?

2 Why was the Royal Navy important for Britain and its empire?

3 Do you agree with the views on splendid isolation given in Source **D**? Give reasons for your answer.

The Anglo-Japanese Alliance

In 1902 Britain and Japan signed an alliance in which they promised to help each other if one of them was attacked by more than one power. This meant that splendid isolation was more splendid than ever. The Boer War ended without any European action against Britain and now Britain had an ally in the Far East to prevent Russian expansion there. Britain did not need any allies in Europe.

Study tip

The Anglo-Japanese Alliance is not named in the specification, so it cannot feature in a question. It is included here to explain splendid isolation, which is named in the specification.

▊ Entente Cordiale

Britain was becoming worried by the size of the German naval fleet. It was not strong enough to challenge Britain, but it could hold the balance of power in any war between Britain and France or Britain and Russia. So, in 1902 Britain put its navy on the 'three-power standard'. This meant that it had to be as large as the next three largest fleets in the world combined. Germany had made it clear that it did not want to ally with either Britain or France, so Britain and France looked to sorting out the problems between them. In 1903–04 the two countries signed the *Entente Cordiale* ('friendly agreement'). In this, France allowed Britain to go ahead with reforms in Egypt and Britain promised not to oppose any French action in Morocco.

The Entente Cordiale was an agreement, not an alliance. Britain had no intention of becoming involved in European affairs. Its colonial problems in Egypt had been solved, its ally Japan was defeating Russia in the Far East and its navy had reached the three-power standard. Germany did not see it this way. It thought that Britain had abandoned isolation and joined France. Germany seemed intent on challenging the Entente Cordiale.

Did you know ??????

The nearest Britain came to a war against a European country at the end of the 19th century was in 1898 at Fashoda in the Sudan. A much smaller French force had to withdraw when faced with the British under Lord Kitchener.

Tasks

4 Which figures in Source **E** represent Britain, France and Germany?

5 What impression of France is the source trying to put forward?

6 What does Source **E** suggest about the Entente Cordiale?

7 Why do you think the Kaiser has his sword showing beneath his overcoat?

8 Do you think this source is a German, French or British view of the Entente Cordiale? Give reasons for your answer.

E *The Entente Cordiale*

Kaiser Wilhelm II's aims in foreign policy

Kaiser Wilhelm II wanted to be in the international limelight. He saw himself as the heroic leader of Germany's army and the founder of a great navy. His wish was to make Germany the greatest nation in the world ('**Weltpolitik**').

Jealous of the British Empire, he set out to give Germany a 'place in the sun'. He tended to upset other countries by his strange habit of making dramatic gestures and statements. This led to him supporting building up the German navy and challenging France in Morocco.

F *An illustration of Kaiser Wilhelm II*

Key terms

Weltpolitik: meaning 'world policy', this phrase is often used to describe Kaiser Wilhelm's desire to be a major player in world affairs.

Key profile

Kaiser Wilhelm II

1859	Born 27 January after a traumatic birth; has a disabled left arm
1877	Joins the army
1881	Marries a Danish princess; they later have seven children
1888	Becomes Kaiser (Emperor) of Germany
1918	Abdicates and flees to Holland
1941	Dies 4 June

Tasks

Look at Sources **F** and **G**.

9 What impression do these images give you of Kaiser Wilhelm II?

10 How accurate do you think they are?

Crisis in Morocco

Morocco in North Africa was one of the few areas of Africa that was not controlled by a European power. As part of the Entente Cordiale, Britain had agreed not to oppose France in its attempts to gain control of Morocco. Germany had the strongest army in the world and claimed the need for Weltpolitik, yet was far behind other European countries in the number of colonies under its rule. Germany decided that it would oppose the French attempt to gain control of Morocco.

In 1905 the Kaiser visited Tangier in Morocco. Although the visit was probably not his idea, he overplayed his part. He rode through the streets of Tangier on a white horse accompanied by a military band and Moroccan troops.

He announced that Germany supported an independent Morocco open to the peaceful competition of all nations for trade and called for an international conference to discuss the future of Morocco. This was typical of the Kaiser and Germany's policy at the beginning of the 20th century. It was a dramatic gesture aimed at preventing France from occupying Morocco and testing the strength of the Entente Cordiale.

G *A drawing of Kaiser Wilhelm II*

The conference was held in 1906 at Algeçiras in southern Spain. Only Austria-Hungary and Morocco supported Germany; Britain and Russia supported France. France had to recognise the independence of Morocco but was given joint control with Spain of the Moroccan police. Germany had failed to prevent France from getting a foothold in Morocco and, even worse, the Entente Cordiale was strengthened. Britain was concerned about Germany's action and began secret military talks with France. Britain had no intention of making a formal alliance with France, but France felt more confident of Britain's support and Britain appeared to be taking more of an interest in European matters.

Study tip

The Kaiser's aims and Germany's aims can be treated as the same. It is important to know what he was trying to do and how this led to the development of alliances and the outbreak of war.

The Anglo-Russian Agreement

Russia and Britain had supported France at Algeçiras and France used its influence to improve relations between them. This led to the signing of an Anglo-Russian Agreement in 1907. This was the solution to several overseas problems for Britain and Russia; especially in Persia and Tibet. Britain now had agreements with France and Russia and this is often referred to as the *Triple Entente*, but no such alliance existed. The Entente Cordiale and the Anglo-Russian Agreement were solutions to colonial problems between France and Britain, and Russia and Britain. They were not military alliances. The Triple Entente was not designed to surround Germany, but unfortunately Germany saw it as part of a policy of encirclement being followed by Britain. Fears like this occurred because the terms of these agreements were secret.

⚭ links

For details on Algeçiras, see page 11.

> **Did you know** ?????
>
> Kaiser Wilhelm II often referred to Britain's policy as one of *Einkreisungspolitik*, which means 'a policy of encirclement'.

> **Study tip**
>
> The Triple Alliance and the Entente Cordiale could appear in a 'describe' question. You need to know which countries are involved in each alliance and the nature of the alliances/agreements.

Tasks

11 How did the Moroccan Crisis of 1905–06 strengthen the Entente Cordiale?

12 Read the paragraph about the Anglo-Russian Agreement.
   a Why did the Anglo-Russian Agreement add to Germany's fears?
   b Do you think these fears were justified? Give reasons for your answer.

The Bosnian Crisis

The next crisis between the powers arose in the Balkans, the area of south-eastern Europe which consisted of many small countries that were in the process of becoming independent from the Turkish Empire. Most of this area was occupied by Slavs. Serbia was the leading Slav state in the Balkans and aimed to unite all the other states under Serbian leadership. Austria-Hungary was also concerned about the Balkans. Austria-Hungary was an empire made up of several different races of people. One of these were the Slavs and Austria-Hungary was worried that they would want to unite with the other Slavs in the Balkans under Serbia. If this happened, many of the other races in Austria-Hungary would also want independence and this could lead to the break-up of the empire of Austria-Hungary.

In 1908 there was a revolution in Turkey. Austria-Hungary took advantage of this to **annex** Bosnia, one of the small Slav states in the Balkans which had been under the control of Turkey. This annoyed Serbia, but it was too small to resist Austria-Hungary, so it appealed to Russia for help. The Russians were annoyed with Austria-Hungary because it had annexed Bosnia without telling them. Russia had long been a supporter of the Slavs, so it backed Serbia's demands for an international conference. Everything depended on the Kaiser.

> **Key terms**
>
> **Annex**: to join or unite; to take possession of.

Wilhelm II was annoyed with Austria-Hungary because it had acted against Bosnia without consulting him, but he still promised it his full support against Russia. This was probably because the agreement that Russia had signed with Britain in 1907 annoyed him even more and he was aware that Austria-Hungary was the only power that had backed Germany at Algeçiras. Russia was too weak to fight and, faced with the opposition of Germany, was forced to back down.

The Bosnian crisis had a great effect on the main powers involved:

- Austria-Hungary now felt it had the full support of Germany, which affected how it acted in 1914.
- Italy did not like Austria-Hungary expanding into the Balkans, so it became less keen on the Triple Alliance.
- Russia had been humiliated by Germany and it was determined that this would not happen again, which led to military improvements in Russia.
- It brought Britain, France and Russia closer together because all of them now had a reason for disliking Germany.
- Serbia had been forced to accept the annexation but was now determined to oppose Austria-Hungary and looked to Russia for further support.

links

See Source **B** on page 7 and note the position of Bosnia and Serbia.

Study tip

You need to know the main details of the Bosnian Crisis because it could occur in a 'describe' question. Equally, it could appear in a bullet-point question on its contribution to the development of the alliances or the outbreak of war.

> 66 Serbia recognises that the annexation of Bosnia by Austria-Hungary has not affected its rights, and consequently it will agree to the decisions of the powers. Serbia undertakes to renounce from now onwards the attitude of protest and opposition which it had adopted with regard to the annexation since last autumn. It undertakes, moreover, to modify the direction of its policy with regard to Austria-Hungary and to live in future on good neighbourly terms with Austria-Hungary. 99

H Note from Austria-Hungary accepted by Serbia after the Bosnian Crisis

Tasks

13   Read Source **H** and explain its meaning.

a   Do you think the Serbs intended to keep the promises they made?

b   As you work through the rest of this chapter make a note of Serbian policies and see if they did behave towards Austria-Hungary as the Serbs had promised in this note.

14   Look back at the first part of this chapter.

a   Make a list of the possible mistakes that Kaiser Wilhelm made in foreign policy.

b   Explain the effect that these mistakes had on the alliances. Did Germany benefit in any way from his policies?

c   Follow this analysis of the Kaiser's policies as you go through the events leading to war.

Agadir: the Second Moroccan Crisis

In 1911 a rebellion against the ruling Sultan broke out in Fez, the capital of Morocco. The Sultan appealed to the French for help and a French army went to Morocco to put down the rebellion. Germany opposed the French action, but did not want to have another defeat over Morocco as it had had in 1906 at Algeçiras. The Germans reacted by sending a gunboat, the *Panther*, to the port of Agadir to protect German interests in Morocco. This seemed fair to the Germans as the French had sent their army to Fez to protect French interests there. They fully expected France to take control of Morocco, but now that Germany had shown some interest, it expected the French to negotiate and Germany would gain something from the talks.

This use of a gunboat was another example of over-reaction by the Germans. It was seen as a warlike action by other countries, especially Britain. It occurred during the naval race with Britain but Germany had not expected that Britain would be interested in their actions in Agadir. The British, however, still annoyed with Germany over the naval race, thought that the Germans were planning to build an Atlantic naval base and use it to challenge Britain's naval base at Gibraltar. This naval action of Germany led to Britain supporting France.

links

See the Crisis in Morocco on page 11.

links

See Anglo-German naval rivalry on page 16.

I *The gunboat* Panther

Did you know ??????

Britain felt obliged to support France in Morocco as they had agreed to in the Entente Cordiale. The British Foreign Secretary, Edward Grey, wrote '*What the French contemplate doing is not wise, but we cannot under our agreement interfere.*'

> But if a situation were to be forced upon us in which peace could only be preserved by the surrender of the great position Britain has won by centuries of heroism and achievement, by allowing Britain to be treated where her interests were vitally affected as if she were of no account in the Cabinet of nations, then I say emphatically that peace at that price would be a humiliation intolerable for a great country like ours to endure.

J Lloyd George's speech at the Mansion House, published in The Times *on 22 July 1911. Lloyd George was then Chancellor of the Exchequer*

Did you know ??????

This speech was seen by Germany as a warning that it could not impose an unreasonable settlement on France.

Preparations for war were made in Germany, Britain and France in 1911, but, in the end, Germany backed down and accepted compensation in the shape of two marshy strips of land in the French Congo in return for accepting French control of Morocco.

The Agadir Crisis was far more dangerous for Europe than the previous crises in Morocco and Bosnia. It brought Europe close to war and affected the relationship between the powers:

- Germany felt humiliated and if there was any future crisis in which German interests were involved, it was unlikely to back down.
- The German people felt more annoyed with Britain than France and German public opinion was beginning to support the idea of a war.
- Britain became more convinced that Germany wanted to dominate Europe.
- Britain reached a secret naval agreement with France. Britain promised to defend the north coast of France if it was attacked from the sea; France promised to defend the Mediterranean.
- Italy opposed Germany over Agadir, which weakened the Triple Alliance and meant Germany relied more on Austria-Hungary.

Tasks

15   What was the effect of the following crises on the alliances?

a   The Bosnian Crisis

b   The Agadir Crisis

16   Read Source **J**.

a   What is Lloyd George suggesting in this source?

b   What effect do you think it would have on France and Germany?

17   How was the Entente Cordiale strengthened by the Agadir Crisis?

18   How was the Triple Alliance changed by the Agadir Crisis?

Study tip

You could be asked to describe the Moroccan Crises, so the details are important, or you could be asked to assess their importance in the formation of the alliances or the outbreak of war.

> 66 *The Second Moroccan Crisis ought to have been called the 'Fez' crisis. The word 'Agadir' shows how much unfavourable limelight the Germans attracted to themselves.* 99

K *The historian W. N. Medlicott writing in 1968*

Tasks

19   What is meant in Source **K** by claiming that the crisis 'ought to have been called the "Fez" crisis'?

20   Why do you think it was called the Agadir Crisis?

21   Which do you think is the better description? Discuss both and explain the reasons for your answer.

Anglo-German naval rivalry

The launch of the first Dreadnought by Britain in 1906 changed the balance of navies in the world. This new battleship was faster and had longer-range guns than older ships. The older ships were now referred to as *fünf Minuten* ships by the Germans because it was estimated that they would last only five minutes if faced by a Dreadnought. Britain's supremacy at sea had been based on the older type of battleship, so its advantage over other navies had been reduced by the launch of the Dreadnought. The power of navies was now measured in how many Dreadnoughts each country had. Other countries imitated the Dreadnought. Germany felt it could now challenge Britain at sea if it had enough Dreadnoughts. This led to the naval race between Britain and Germany.

> **Did you know** ??????
>
> 'Dreadnought' literally means 'fears nothing', or 'fearless'.

> **Did you know** ??????
>
> The first 'Dreadnought' was the British battleship HMS *Dreadnought* – it had such an impact that, after its launch, similar battleships built were all referred to as 'Dreadnoughts'.

L *HMS Dreadnought, 1909*

M *The naval race: numbers of Dreadnoughts, 1906–14*

Year	Britain	Germany
1906	1	0
1907	3	0
1908	2	4
1909	2	3
1910	3	1
1911	5	3
1912	3	2
1913	7	3
1914	3	1
Total	29	17

The importance of the navy to Britain is explained on page 8. It played a vital part in Britain making agreements with France and Russia. In 1909 the Germans were believed to be speeding up their production of Dreadnoughts. Public opinion in Britain became alarmed by this. There was a belief that the only reason that Germany was increasing its fleet was that it wanted to dominate Britain and Europe. Britain was planning to build four Dreadnoughts in 1909, but there were demands for this to be doubled by groups who wanted to increase spending on the navy, using the slogan 'we want eight and won't wait'. The Agadir Crisis of 1911 increased Britain's fears of Germany's aims and, for the first time, the possibility of a war against Germany became a reality.

After 1911 the naval race continued but it was less intense because Britain had gone further ahead. Germany did not seem to realise the threat that its navy was to Britain. Germany was a Great Power because of its army, whereas Britain depended on its navy for its position as a Great Power. The naval rivalry did not directly cause the war, but it did mean that, if a war came, Britain was likely to fight against Germany.

> 66 *A German fleet is a luxury not a national necessity.* 99

N *Winston Churchill, First Lord of the Admiralty, speaking in 1912*

> 66 *Building a battle-fleet was necessary if we wanted to become a sea-power. Sea power was needed to protect trade, as other states had realised long before we did. Our surrounded and threatened position convinced me that no time was to be lost in turning ourselves into a sea-power.* 99

O *Admiral von Tirpitz writing in his memoirs. Von Tirpitz was the member of the German government in charge of the navy*

> 66 *I had a peculiar passion for the navy. It sprang to no small extent from my English blood. When I was a little boy I admired the proud British ships. There awoke in me the will to build ships of my own like these some day, and when I was grown up to possess a fine navy as the English.* 99

P *Adapted from the autobiography of Kaiser Wilhelm II,* My Early Life

Tasks

22 In which year does Source **M** suggest that Britain was pulling ahead of Germany in the naval race?

23 Why was Britain so concerned about Germany building a navy?

24 What did Churchill mean in Source **N**?

25 What effect do you think the German navy had on Britain's relations with Germany? Give reasons for your answer.

26 Read Source **O**.

a Explain von Tirpitz's reasons for building the German navy.

b Why do you think he made this statement?

c How does von Tirpitz's statement differ from Churchill's in Source **N**?

27 Read Source **P**.

a What reasons does the Kaiser give for building a navy?

b What purpose could he have for making this statement?

The arms race

By 1907 Europe had been divided up into two armed camps: the Triple Alliance and the Triple Entente. All the alliances were defensive but, as they were secret, this was not known. Therefore, all countries involved feared that each alliance was directed against them. Germany felt that the Entente Cordiale powers were trying to surround Germany; France and Russia felt that Germany was trying to expand its territory towards them. The fears and crises that these alliances caused also led to countries building up their armies.

⚭ links

See Britain's policy of encirclement on page 12.

Q *Size of the armies in Europe (in millions), 1900–14*

Country	1900	1910	1914
France	0.7	0.8	1.0
Britain	0.5	0.5	0.4
Russia	1.1	1.3	1.5
Austria-Hungary	0.25	0.3	0.48
Germany	0.5	0.7	0.8
Italy	0.25	0.3	0.35

Note: the figures for 1914 relate to the number of soldiers that could be mobilised at that time.

R *Cartoon showing Wilhelm II telling Polish soldiers that they will not regret dedicating their lives to him. Cartoon from the French magazine 'L'assiette au Beurre' c. 1910–12*

Tasks

28 Compare the build-up of armies in the table in Source **Q**.

 a Which country's army increased the least during this period? Suggest reasons for this.

 b Which country had the greatest percentage increase in its army between 1900 and 1914?

29 Study Source **R**.

 a What is the cartoon suggesting about the Kaiser?

 b What evidence is there that this source is accurate in its view of the Kaiser?

 c What does the source suggest that the French should be doing?

Study tip

The arms race is normally given as proof of Germany's aggressive intentions, but could it have been defensive? You could be asked to describe the naval race or to assess the effect of the arms race on the development of the alliances or the outbreak of war.

1.2 Why did war break out in 1914?

The assassination of Archduke Franz Ferdinand

A closer look

Franz Ferdinand visited Sarajevo on 28 June 1914. This was a national festival day for the Serbs, so feeling against the visit was high. In spite of this, security measures were poor. There were only 120 police to cover a journey of 6 km. The police were supposed to face the crowd, but many of them became over-excited when the procession of six cars including the Archduke's came into sight so they turned to face the parade. One of the assassins, Cabrinovic, threw a hand grenade at the Archduke's car, which deflected off the Archduke's arm and fell into the road, wounding around 20 people.

The decision was made to continue the parade. Arrangements were made for the cavalcade to detour so that the Archduke could visit the wounded in hospital, but no one told the Archduke's driver. When he turned in the wrong direction, he was ordered to stop. The car came to a halt in front of Gavrilo Princip, who was just coming out of a sandwich shop. Princip took out his gun and fired two shots. One hit the Archduke; the other hit the Archduke's wife, Sophie. Sophie died 15 minutes later and Franz Ferdinand shortly afterwards.

The assassins were put on trial and two of them were executed. Princip was only 19 and too young for the death penalty, so he was imprisoned for 20 years. He died in prison in 1918.

Did you know ??????

The Sarajevo assassins were all Bosnians and therefore subjects of Austria-Hungary. Austria-Hungary blamed Serbia because the Black Hand had supplied their weapons. The Black Hand is described in more detail in the next section.

Tasks

1 How good were the security measures set up to protect Franz Ferdinand? Give reasons to support your answer.

2 Why do you think Austria-Hungary was annoyed by the assassination?

3 Who do think Austria-Hungary would blame?

Study tip

You could be asked to describe the assassination, but you are more likely to be asked to assess its role in the outbreak of war.

A The arrest of Gavrilo Princip

 I am a Yugoslav nationalist and aim at the union of all Slavs and their deliverance from Austria. "

B Gavrilo Princip at his trial

The Balkans

To understand the reasons for the assassination, it is necessary to examine the aims of those involved. Serbia and Russia had been forced to back down by the German support given to Austria-Hungary over Bosnia in 1908–09. Russia built up its armed forces and Serbia was enlarged after victory in the 1912–13 Balkan Wars. Austria-Hungary was concerned by the success of Serbia and was looking for an excuse to defeat it and prevent the break-up of the Austro-Hungarian Empire. Serbia still aimed for the creation of a Greater Serbia and saw its success in the Balkan Wars as the first step to this.

At the end of the Balkan Wars, Serbia was the strongest of the Balkan countries. Many Serbs living in Bosnia were unhappy with the rule of Austria-Hungary. Bosnia was seen by many in Serbia as the next area of expansion when they had recovered from the Balkan Wars.

In 1911 ten men formed the Black Hand in Serbia. This group was a secret society aimed at uniting all Serbs in a Greater Serbia. By 1914 it had around 2,500 members, some of whom were leading officials in the Serb army. To show their opposition to Austria-Hungary, they planned to assassinate Archduke Franz Ferdinand, the heir to the Austro-Hungarian throne, when he visited Sarajevo in Bosnia in 1914.

C *The seal of the Black Hand movement*

Did you know ??????

The stated aim of the Black Hand was 'To realise the national ideal, the unification of all Serbs. This organisation prefers terrorist action to cultural activities; it will therefore remain secret.'

Tasks

4 What were the aims of Austria-Hungary and Serbia in the Balkans?

5 Compare the aims of the Black Hand and Serbia. How were they the same and how were they different?

∞ **links**

See the Bosnian Crisis on page 12 and Source **B** on page 7.

The events leading to war in 1914

Most countries in Europe thought the assassination of Franz Ferdinand was a local matter that would be solved by negotiations between Austria-Hungary and Serbia. This did not happen because of the determination of the Austro-Hungarian war party to take revenge on Serbia and the role of the alliances. It is highly unlikely that the assassination was an attempt by Serbia to cause war with Austria-Hungary. Serbia had just been involved in the Balkan Wars and needed time to recover before even considering a war against Austria-Hungary.

The leader of the war party in Austria-Hungary was Conrad von Hötzendorf, the leader of the Austrian army and a close friend of Archduke Franz Ferdinand. Between the beginning of 1913 and June 1914, Conrad had proposed a war against Serbia 25 times. He felt that the future of Austria-Hungary depended on crushing Serbia.

Timeline

1914: from assassination to war

28 Jun	Assassination of Archduke Franz Ferdinand
6 Jul	Germany promises support to Austria-Hungary
23 Jul	Austro-Hungarian ultimatum to Serbia
24 Jul	Russia offers support to Serbia
28 Jul	Austria-Hungary declares war on Serbia
30 Jul	Russia begins to mobilise its forces
1 Aug	Germany declares war on Russia
3 Aug	Germany declares war on France; German troops enter Belgium
4 Aug	Germany declares war on Belgium; Britain declares war on Germany
5 Aug	France declares war on Germany
6 Aug	Austria-Hungary declares war on Russia

The assassination of the Archduke was the perfect excuse for dealing with Serbia. His message to the politicians of Austria-Hungary after the assassination was direct to the point (Source **D**).

> 66 *This is not the crime of a single fanatic; assassination represents Serbia's declaration of war on Austria-Hungary. If we miss this occasion, Austria-Hungary will be faced with new demands of independence from South Slavs, Czechs, Russians, Rumanians and Italians living within Austria-Hungary. Austria-Hungary must wage war against Serbia for political reasons.* 99

 D *Conrad von Hötzendorf, 1914*

Austria-Hungary sent a 10-point **ultimatum** to Serbia. Serbia accepted all but one of the 10 points. Point 6 would have involved Austrians influencing the justice system in Serbia, so the Serbs could not accept it. However, they were prepared to refer the matter to the International Court at The Hague or to the other Great Powers. Serbia expected that this would satisfy Austria-Hungary or at least lead to negotiations. Many Germans also thought that the Serbian response was favourable. However, the Austrians, having been assured of Germany's support on 6 July, felt confident that this was their opportunity to deal with the problem of Serbia. They declared war on Serbia on 28 July.

This declaration of war triggered off the alliances and led to the outbreak of the First World War. Russia had let down Serbia over Bosnia in 1908–09 and was determined not to let it down again. On 30 July Russia began to **mobilise** its forces against Austria-Hungary and Germany. Germany then declared war on Russia on 1 August. At this stage, the war only involved the east of Europe. It was the Schlieffen Plan – Germany's plan for war – that ensured it spread to the west.

> 66 *Although the horrible murder was the work of a Serbian society with branches all over the country, many details prove that the Serbian government had neither instigated it nor desired it. The Serbs were exhausted by two wars. The most hot-headed among them might have paused at the thought of war with Austria-Hungary who was overwhelmingly superior to Serbia.* 99

E *From the memoirs of German Chancellor von Bülow*

Key terms

Ultimatum: a final demand with a threat of force if you do not agree.

Mobilise: to get troops ready for war.

Did you know ??????

Point 6 which Serbia could not accept was: 'To open a judicial inquiry against those implicated in the murder, and to allow delegates of Austria-Hungary to take part in this.'

Did you know ??????

On 6 July, Wilhelm II told Austria-Hungary that Germany would support whatever action it took against Serbia – in effect, offering it a 'blank cheque'.

Did you know ??????

The Austrians declared war on Serbia by telegram. This was the first time in history that this method had been used to declare war.

Tasks

6 Read Source **D**. Explain fully Conrad von Hötzendorf's reasons for wanting Austria-Hungary to declare war on Serbia.

7 Do you think point 6 of the ultimatum to Serbia was reasonable? Give reasons for your answer.

8 If German opinion was as stated in Source **E**, why did the German government give full support to Austria-Hungary?

The Schlieffen Plan

Since 1893 when the Franco-Russian Alliance was signed, Germany had a problem of what to do in the event of a war on two fronts – that is, if France attacked them from the west and Russia from the east.

In 1905 the German head of the army, von Schlieffen, decided that the best way to deal with this problem was to attack the French first and defeat them within six weeks. The French would be expecting an attack in Alsace-Lorraine where they shared a border with Germany. Schlieffen reasoned that the French would not expect an attack in the north where they had a border with **neutral** Belgium. If the German army attacked through neutral Holland and Belgium, the French would be taken by surprise and the speed of the German attack would lead to France surrendering in six weeks.

Schlieffen argued that Russia would take a long time to mobilise because of the size and backwardness of the country, so Germany would be able to defeat France quickly and then use the same armies in the east to defeat Russia. Schlieffen had died in 1912, but it was his plan – slightly changed so that they only attacked through Belgium not Holland – that the Germans used in 1914. For it to succeed, the attack on France had to be swift.

Key terms

Neutral: a country that favours neither side in a dispute or war.

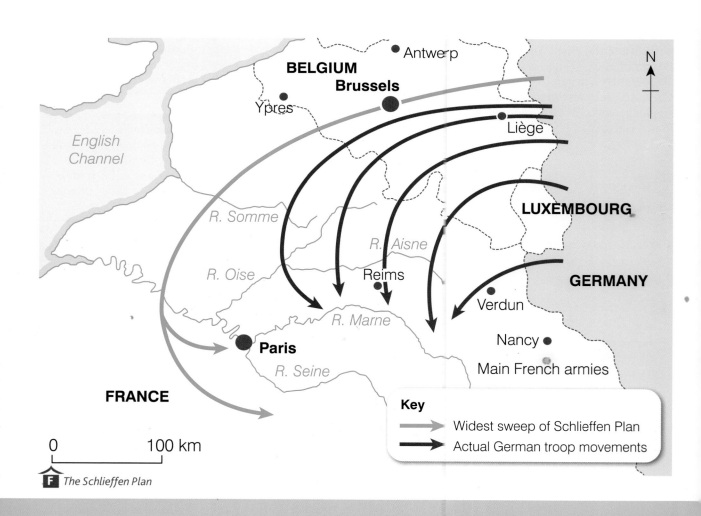

Key

→ Widest sweep of Schlieffen Plan
→ Actual German troop movements

0   100 km

F *The Schlieffen Plan*

Britain had no intention of joining the war in support of Russia against Austria-Hungary. There is no certainty that Britain would have helped France if Germany had attacked from Alsace. Britain's main concern was its own security. It did not want a strong power in control of the coast of Western Europe because it was afraid that an attack on Britain could be launched from here. This is why it had promised to protect the north coast of France in 1912. Moreover, Belgium had been declared a neutral country by the Treaty of London in 1839. Britain had signed this treaty along with the other leading European countries including Prussia (part of Germany in 1914). When German troops entered Belgium as part of the Schlieffen Plan on 3 August, Britain declared war on Germany. Britain claimed to be going to war to protect the sanctity of treaties. The Kaiser was surprised that Britain was prepared to fight over what he called 'a scrap of paper'.

links

The agreement to protect the northern coast of France was a result of the second Moroccan Crisis, see pages 14 and 15.

Did you know ??????

Officially, the declaration of war meant that 'a state of war exists between Great Britain and Germany as from 11pm on August 4, 1914'.

G *Recruitment poster used in Britain, highlighting the 'scrap of paper'*

Task

9   Why did Germany attack Belgium in 1914?

Hint

Use Source **F** as well as the text.

Task

10   Do you think Britain went to war to protect the sanctity of treaties? Explain your answer.

Activities

These activities could be completed as a discussion, debate, group work, role-play or simply to plan an argument from different points of view.

1 Read the following statements which refer to each of the powers involved in the outbreak of the First World War.

 a   Britain was the most responsible for the outbreak of war because it tried to encircle Germany and did not make it clear to Germany that it would go to war over Belgium.

 b   France was the most responsible for the outbreak of war because it wanted revenge against Germany and to get back Alsace and Lorraine.

 c   Germany was the most responsible for the outbreak of war because of its aggressive policies and the support it gave to Austria-Hungary in 1914.

 d   Austria-Hungary was the most responsible for the outbreak of war because it refused to negotiate with Serbia.

 e   Serbia was the most responsible for the outbreak of war because it was responsible for the assassination of Archduke Franz Ferdinand.

 f   Russia was the most responsible for the outbreak of war because it mobilised in support of Serbia.

2 Get as much evidence as you can to support and oppose each of the above statements.

3 Using the evidence you have obtained, make a list of the powers, putting the country you feel was most responsible at the top of the list, followed by the next and so on, until at the bottom is the country that you consider was the least responsible.

4 Explain why you have listed the countries in this order.

Study tip

The Schlieffen Plan is important because it brought the war to Western Europe. You need to be able to explain how and why it contributed to the outbreak of war in the West.

Study tip

In the extended writing question, you will be asked to assess the relative importance of two bullet points to an issue such as the outbreak of the First World War. The bullet points will always be topics named in the specification such as the alliance system, Germany's aims, Morocco, Bosnia and the Balkans, the arms race, the assassination of Franz Ferdinand, the Schlieffen Plan, or any of the countries that contributed to the outbreak of war.

Practice questions

Study **Source A** and then answer all three questions that follow.

Source A British cartoon published in 1905 making fun of German arrogance
at the Entente Cordiale between France and Britain

1   From 1906 to 1914 there was naval rivalry between Britain and Germany.
Describe the naval race between the two countries.   *(4 marks)*

2   **Source A** suggests reasons for Britain ending its splendid isolation by making the
Entente Cordiale with France in 1904.

Do you agree that these were the main reasons for ending splendid isolation?

Explain your answer by referring to the purpose of the source as well as using its
content and your knowledge.   *(6 marks)*

3   Which was the more important reason for the outbreak of the First World War
in 1914:

- the Moroccan Crises 1905 and 1911;
- the assassination at Sarajevo in 1914?

You must refer to **both** reasons when explaining your answer.   *(10 marks)*

2.1 How did the Treaty of Versailles establish peace?

A *The peacemakers, May 1919: Lloyd George, Orlando, Clemenceau and Wilson*

Objectives

In this chapter you will learn about:

the aims of the peacemakers at the Paris Peace Conference

the terms, strengths and weaknesses of the Treaty of Versailles

the aims, organisation, membership and powers of the League of Nations

crises facing the League of Nations in Manchuria and Abyssinia

why the League of Nations failed.

The war against Germany ended with the armistice on 11 November 1918. The Entente Cordiale powers had defeated Germany, but at a price. In the West the war had been fought mostly in France and Belgium and much of their land had been devastated. Military losses for Britain and the empire totalled around 1 million, for France they were around 1.4 million and for the USA just over 100,000. Added to this were the wounded, which came to about 20 million, and civilian losses which totalled over 6 million if the influenza epidemic of 1918–19 is included. It is no surprise that there was a lot of ill feeling in 1918 against both war and Germany. It was feelings like this that led to the Treaty of Versailles and the establishment of the League of Nations. Why did they fail?

Timeline

From armistice to Abyssinia

Jan	1918	Wilson's Fourteen Points published
Nov	1918	Armistice signed by Germany
Jan	1919	Peacemakers meet in Paris; influenza epidemic in Europe
Jun	1919	Treaty of Versailles
Nov	1919	USA votes not to join the League
Apr	1921	Reparations figure set
	1926	Germany joins the League
	1929	Wall Street Crash
	1931	Manchurian Crisis
	1933	Japan and Germany leave the League
	1935	Abyssinian Crisis

The Paris Peace Conference

The delegates of 32 states attended the Paris Peace Conference. None of the defeated powers attended the conference, nor did Russia which was in the middle of a civil war. The main decisions were taken by the 'Big Three': Clemenceau of France, Wilson of the USA and Lloyd George of Britain. The aims of these three were different and it is important to consider them to understand the final treaty that resulted.

Georges Clemenceau

Clemenceau was 78 in 1919. He had seen Germany invade France twice in his lifetime, in 1870 and 1914, and was under great pressure from the French public who wanted revenge on Germany. Most of the war had been fought on French soil and the industry and agriculture of north-west France had been virtually ruined. The desire of the French people for revenge and compensation was understandable but unlikely to lead to a fair peace agreement. Clemenceau's main aim at the conference was to gain security for France by preventing another attack on its frontiers. This involved keeping Germany weak and making it difficult for it to recover. He aimed to do this by disarming the Germans, regaining Alsace and Lorraine and making Germany pay the cost of the damage France had suffered during the war.

B *Cartoon showing Clemenceau triumphant over Germany*

Key profile	
Georges Clemenceau	
1841	Born 28 September; nicknamed 'the tiger'
1906	Elected Prime Minister of France
1909	Resigns as Prime Minister
1917	Elected again as Prime Minister in order to win the war
1920	Loses power because the treaty was too lenient
1929	Dies 24 November

David Lloyd George

David Lloyd George had led Britain to victory in the First World War. At the end of 1918 he won a very convincing victory in the general election. In this election campaign, his party had used slogans such as 'Hang the Kaiser' and 'Make Germany Pay'. There was a massive press campaign in Britain for the punishment of Germany. Lloyd George did not share these views. His main aims were to preserve the supremacy of the British navy and to prevent a settlement that was so harsh it would not work because Germany would never accept it. He was afraid that if Germany was punished too harshly, the German people may turn to Communism. He also realised that Britain depended on trade for its wealth, so the recovery of the German economy was important for Britain. For these reasons, Lloyd George was the compromise view at the Paris Peace Conference between the extreme Clemenceau and the more moderate Woodrow Wilson.

Key profile

David Lloyd George

1863	Born 17 January
1890	Elected to parliament
1908	Appointed Chancellor of the Exchequer
1911	Makes Mansion House speech
1916	Becomes Prime Minister
1922	Resigns as Prime Minister
1945	Dies 26 March

> 66 'I have personally no doubt that we will get everything out of her that you can squeeze out of a lemon and a bit more.' 99
>
> *Sir Eric Geddes, a member of Lloyd George's cabinet, speaking at Cambridge on 9 December*

> 66 'We propose to demand the whole cost of the war from Germany. Germany must pay to the last farthing.' 99
>
> *Lloyd George, speaking at Bristol on 11 December*

C Speeches from the 1918 general election campaign

Woodrow Wilson

The US President had published his fourteen-point plan during the war in January 1918. Germany showed no interest in it and carried on fighting. In fact, the German leaders showed that they had little time for the principles of the Fourteen Points when they made peace with Russia by the Treaty of Brest-Litovsk in March 1918. Russia was forced to give up a large amount of land to Germany and Austria-Hungary and to pay an enormous **war indemnity**. This gave the Allies some idea of how Germany would treat the defeated nations if it had been victorious in the war. It was only when the Germans had been defeated and their allies had deserted them that they showed an interest in the Fourteen Points. They claimed that they believed that they had agreed to peace on the basis of these points.

Wilson was an idealist who believed that lasting peace was not possible without the introduction of new standards into public life. He believed that countries should be open and truthful with each other and that the boundaries of Europe should be reorganised according to the principle of **self-determination**. The USA had only been in the war since 1917 and Wilson did not appreciate the strong feelings against Germany that existed in France and Britain, so he simplified the problems. Moreover, it soon became obvious that his party was losing support in the USA and there was a growing feeling in America that the USA should have nothing to do with Europe. There was no certainty that the USA would sign the treaty. As the conference went on, Wilson began to give in more to the views of Clemenceau, putting all his faith in the success of the League of Nations – the last of his Fourteen Points.

Tasks

1. What were the main problems facing Clemenceau, Lloyd George and Wilson at the Paris Peace Conference?

2. Read Source **C**.
   a. How do the speeches suggest that Germany should be punished for the First World War?
   b. Why do you think the speeches are asking for so much?

Hint

For Task 2a, consider the audience (i.e. to whom they are speaking) and the purpose of the source.

Key terms

War indemnity: a sum of money that a country is forced to pay if it is defeated in war.

Self-determination: the right of all people to decide which country they will be ruled by.

Die Grundlage für den Völkerbund

„Nur so kann Deutschland darin geduldet werden!"

D *David Lloyd George, Georges Clemenceau and Woodrow Wilson as avenging angels standing on a dead body representing Germany. The text beneath the cartoon means 'The only way Germany can be tolerated'*

Some of the Fourteen Points:

1   *The end of secret treaties.*

2   *Freedom of the seas.*

3   *Removal of all customs duties.*

4   *Reduction in armies and weapons.*

5   *Future of colonies to be decided fairly.*

6   *German troops to leave Russia.*

7   *Belgium to be restored to independence.*

8   *Alsace and Lorraine to go back to France.*

10   *People of Austria-Hungary to be given independence.*

11   *Serbia to be restored.*

13   *An independent Poland to be set up with a port.*

14   *The formation of an association of nations to guarantee peace.*

E

Key profile

Woodrow Wilson

1856	Born 28 December to a devout Presbyterian family
1910	Becomes Democratic Governor of New Jersey
1912	Elected President
1914	Declares American neutrality in war
1916	Re-elected President
1917	Takes the USA into war
1918	Publishes the Fourteen Points
	Democrats gain control of US Congress
1919	Awarded Nobel Peace Prize
	Suffers a stroke
1921	Warren G. Harding, a Republican, becomes President
1924	Dies 3 February

Did you know ??????

Woodrow Wilson is the only US President who has been awarded a Doctor of Philosophy in government and history.

Task

3   Study Source **D**.

a   Explain the meaning of the picture.

b   Which country do you think was responsible for the publication of this source? Give reasons for your answer.

Did you know ??????

The Fourteen Points were originally part of a speech given by Wilson in January 1918 to reassure the USA that the World War was being fought for a moral cause and to ensure lasting peace in Europe.

4 Read Source **E**.

a Which of the Fourteen Points do you think France would have supported and which would they oppose? Explain your answer.

b Which of the Fourteen Points do you think Britain would have objected to the most? Explain why.

5 Explain why Germany wanted the peace to be based on the Fourteen Points.

6 Explain the meaning of Source **F**. How far does it explain the differences between the aims of Wilson and Clemenceau at the conference?

> 66 *Wilson: Monsieur Clemenceau, have you ever been to Germany?*
> *Clemenceau: No, sir! But twice in my lifetime the Germans have been to France.* 99

F A conversation between Wilson and Clemenceau at the Paris Peace Conference

Study tip

It is important to know the aims of the Big Three at the conference and to be able to explain why they were so different.

The terms of the Treaty of Versailles

When the peacemakers had finished their discussion at Paris, they went to the Palace of Versailles. Here, the German delegates were forced to sign the Treaty of Versailles on 28 June 1919. This treaty dealt only with Germany.

The first 26 clauses of the treaty were the Covenant of the League of Nations, which will be covered later. Wilson had insisted on the inclusion of the League as he thought that this would be able to modify some of the extremes of the treaty later.

links

See page 36 for the Covenant of the League of Nations.

Did you know ??????

The Hall of Mirrors was also where the German Emperor William I was crowned after Prussia had defeated France in the Franco Prussian War 1870–71, creating Germany from lots of smaller states. This unification was the root of many of the problems that had caused the First World War.

G The Hall of Mirrors at the Palace of Versailles

The Treaty of Versailles punished Germany in the following ways.

Loss of land

On the western frontier of Germany:

- Alsace and Lorraine were restored to France.
- The provinces of Eupen and Malmedy were given to Belgium after **plebiscites**.
- North Schleswig was transferred to Denmark after a plebiscite.
- The Saar Coalfield was put under the control of the League of Nations for 15 years and France was allowed to take the coal during that time. After 15 years there was to be a plebiscite.

> **Key terms**
>
> **Plebiscite:** a vote by the people on a question of national importance.
>
> **Mandate:** the power to rule a country granted by the League in preparation for self-government.

H *Germany's loss of territory under the Treaty of Versailles*

On the eastern frontier of Germany:

- An independent Poland which had been destroyed in the 18th century was restored.
- The port of Danzig was made a free city under the control of the League of Nations. Danzig had a mainly German population, but Poland needed it as an outlet to the sea for trade.
- Upper Silesia was divided between Germany and Poland after a plebiscite.
- The port of Memel was to be ruled by the League. It was taken by Lithuania in 1923.
- All the gains that Germany had made from the defeat of Russia in 1918 were given up, mostly to Poland but also to form the independent states of Estonia, Latvia and Lithuania.
- The union of Austria and Germany (Anschluss) was forbidden.
- All Germany's colonies were surrendered and given to the victorious powers as **mandates** by the League of Nations.

> **Study tip**
>
> There were five treaties in all, including the Treaties of St Germain and Trianon which divided Austria-Hungary, but you will only be examined on the Treaty of Versailles.

Study Map **H** and consider the land lost by Germany.

1. In groups, discuss Germany's feelings about the loss of land. Make a list of those points that seemed to be fair and those that were not.

2. Do you think Germany was justified in objecting to losing any of the land in the treaty?

3. Would you have changed the territorial settlement in any way?

4. Do you think any other countries would have objected to your settlement? Explain why.

Military restrictions

- The army was limited to 100,000 men. **Conscription** was not allowed and tanks and military aircraft were forbidden.
- The navy was limited to 15,000 men and to have only 6 battleships and no submarines.
- The Rhineland was declared to be a demilitarised zone. This meant that although it still belonged to Germany, no German troops or weapons were to be allowed within 50 km of the river Rhine. Allied troops were to occupy part of this area for 15 years, although they had all left by 1930.

Did you know ??????

Even armoured cars were forbidden under the terms of demilitarisation!

War guilt

Germany was forced to accept that it was guilty of causing the war. This was included to give the Allies a legal reason for demanding the payment of **reparations** from Germany. It also was a moral condemnation of the actions of the country.

> ❝ The Allied governments affirm and Germany accepts the responsibility of Germany and her allies for causing all the loss and damage to which the Allies have been subjected as a result of the war imposed on them by the aggression of Germany and her allies. ❞

I Clause 231 of the treaty – the war guilt clause

Did you know ??????

Reparations also included payment with products such as coal and steel, and the patent for aspirin.

Reparations

The idea of reparations, that is the defeated powers paying the victorious powers the cost of the war, was not new. In 1871 Germany had forced France to pay £200 million for the cost of a war that had lasted for less than a year and was fought almost entirely in France. As recently as March 1917, Germany had charged Russia a large war indemnity when it was forced to make peace after a war, much of which had been fought on Russian soil. If France and its one-time ally Russia had been treated so harshly by Germany, how much would France expect Germany to pay for a war that had been fought over four years and mostly in France and Belgium, not Germany?

The war had been costly for everyone: all the countries involved had lost large numbers of men and spent a vast amount of money on munitions, transport and supplies for the fighting men. In the case of France and Belgium, in addition to their losses of men and weapons, much of their land and industry had been destroyed by the war. The problem of reparations was so complex that it was too difficult to solve in 1919. Feelings of hatred and revenge in the victorious countries against the defeated ones were too great. A Reparations Commission was set up, which reported in 1921; reparations were set at £6,600 million. Germany was originally given 42 years to pay, but the amount was reduced in 1929 and it stopped paying in the 1930s.

Task

7   Review the aims of Clemenceau, Lloyd George and Wilson. How far did each of them achieve their aims in the Treaty of Versailles? Whom of the three do you think would be most satisfied with the treaty? Give reasons for your answer.

Germany's objections to the Treaty of Versailles

Diktat

When the clauses of the Treaty of Versailles had been decided, Germany expected to be able to negotiate the terms. In fact, it was given three weeks to protest and only minor details were changed as a result of these protests. This lack of negotiation led to the German people referring to the treaty as the *Diktat* of Versailles. Many Germans, like Hitler, felt that because they had not been involved in drawing up the terms of the treaty, they did not have to keep to them. However, could they have expected any better treatment after the way they had forced a diktat in the Treaty of Brest-Litovsk with Russia in 1917?

Loss of land

In Europe, Germany had lost 72,500 km² of land and between 6 and 7 million people. This was over 10 per cent of its land and people. In Eastern Europe, 1.5 million German-speaking people had been placed under the control of Poland. Lloyd George opposed this and argued that this would lead to future war. Germany was annoyed because it was against the principle of self-determination – one of the Fourteen Points. In addition, the Polish Corridor, whose inhabitants were mostly Poles, gave Poland access to the sea but separated Germany from its province of East Prussia. The distribution of its colonies to the victorious powers was not seen as fair by Germany.

Key terms

Diktat: 'dictated peace' – the Germans called the treaty this because Germany was forced to sign it.

∞ links

For the Treaty of Brest-Litovsk, see page 28.

Did you know ??????

Britain took the majority of Germany's colonies, including Cameroon and most of German East Africa. German Samoa and German New Guinea were given to New Zealand and Australia, which were part of the British Empire. Many German colonies also went to France and Belgium.

Military restrictions

Germany had always taken pride in its armed forces and claimed that an army of 100,000 was not only too small to defend itself but also not even enough to keep order inside Germany. Moreover, the Fourteen Points mentioned disarmament for all, but by 1919 only Germany had reduced its forces.

The demilitarisation of the Rhineland was to protect France. Clemenceau had wanted the Rhineland to be set up as an independent state controlled by France, but he had been forced to accept that it stayed German because Germans lived there.

War guilt

The German people felt that they had been blamed for what the Kaiser and other countries had done. The Kaiser no longer ruled Germany and a new democratic government had been set up. Germany claimed that it was unfair to blame the new government for the behaviour of the previous one. They were disgraced and humiliated by this clause, although the democratic government was only set up after the war had been lost.

Reparations

The amount set for reparations was far too much for Germany to pay. The war had been costly to Germany as well as the Allies, and it had lost industrial land in the treaty. France was not interested in how much Germany could afford, but wanted reparations to ruin the German economy so that it could never again attack France. Lloyd George realised that trade in Europe depended on Germany recovering economically. The longer reparations went on, the longer it would take for trade to recover and the longer it would take for the bitterness of the war to disappear.

> **Did you know** ??????
>
> Before the war, Germany had been the biggest economic power in Europe, exporting more goods than any other country in the world except the USA.

◼ Strengths and weaknesses of the Treaty of Versailles

The Treaty of Versailles brought peace to Europe and set up an international organisation, the League of Nations, to preserve the peace. However, it left Germany with many grievances, some of which seemed justified because some of the terms of the treaty contradicted the Fourteen Points.

If Germany ever recovered from the war, it would be determined to get rid of what it saw as the unfair parts of the treaty. This could lead to future problems. President Wilson had put too much faith in the power of the League of Nations to solve these problems. When the US government refused to sign the treaty and did not join the League, the whole settlement became less secure.

> **Did you know** ??????
>
> In some ways, the treaty was lenient towards Germany: Austria-Hungary was split up at the end of the war, whereas Germany remained as one country with a population of around 60 million compared to 40 million in France. Perhaps this was the greatest weakness of the treaty.

J *German cartoon from 1919 on the Treaty of Versailles*

Tasks

8 Which terms of the Treaty of Versailles do you think were unfair on Germany? Explain your answer.

9 Which of the terms of the treaty was Germany most upset by? Give reasons and refer to all the terms in your answer.

10 Study Source **J**.

a Which country is the condemned man meant to represent?

b Do you recognise the other three figures in the cartoon? Name them.

c Explain the meaning of the source. How accurate do you think it is about the Treaty of Versailles?

Why did the League of Nations fail in its attempt to keep peace?

Membership

It was presumed that most of the victorious countries would join the League of Nations because the aim of the League was for countries to join together to prevent war. When the USA did not sign the Treaty of Versailles and did not join the League, it was weakened. Moreover, Germany was not allowed to join so it regarded it as a 'League of victors' and Russia (named the USSR from 1923) was not invited to join. This meant that the League got off to a bad start.

Did you know ??????

The League of Nations had 42 founder members. At its largest, between September 1934 and February 1935, there were 58 member states.

Covenant of the League

This was the 26 articles of the League that all member states had to agree to. It was meant to improve international cooperation, peace and security. It included:

- the compulsory registration of all treaties to avoid further secret alliances
- the reduction and control of arms so that there could be no future arms race
- a method of solving disputes between countries known as **collective security**.

In this way, it dealt with all the reasons that people felt had caused the First World War.

A *The opening of the League of Nations in Geneva, 1920*

Key terms

Collective security: if one state attacked another, all the members would join together and act against the aggressor.

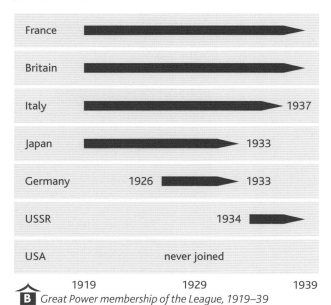

B *Great Power membership of the League, 1919–39*

Organisation of the League

The Assembly

Each member nation was represented on the Assembly, which met once a year to discuss general topics such as the revision of treaties and the admission of new members. All decisions had to be unanimous.

The Council

This consisted of five permanent members, which was reduced to four when the USA did not sign the covenant. These were Britain, France, Italy and Japan. They were joined by four (initially) non-permanent members who were elected for a three-year period. The Council's main duty was to solve any disputes that might occur between states, by negotiation if possible. If any country was considered to have started a war by an act of aggression, then that war became the concern of all the countries in the League who would take action against the aggressor. This action was in three stages:

- Moral condemnation: this meant that all countries would put pressure on the aggressor in order to shame that country into stopping the war and accepting the League's decision.
- Economic sanctions: all countries in the League would stop trading with the aggressor.
- Military force: all countries in the League would contribute to an armed force that would act against the aggressor.

In this way, the Council was to provide the machinery to enforce the principle of collective security which would guarantee future peace.

The Permanent Court of Justice

This was a court of 15 judges chosen from the nations of the League and set up at The Hague in the Netherlands. It dealt with disputes between countries over international law such as the terms of treaties. It had no means of enforcing its decisions, so it depended on the goodwill of the members.

Weaknesses of the League

The withdrawal of the USA and the exclusion of Germany and Russia from the League seriously weakened it from the start. The major powers in the League in 1920 were Britain and France, neither of whom was prepared to play a leading role. The Secretariat looked after the day-to-day business of the League, but the machinery of the organisation had several weaknesses. Each member of the Council had the right of **veto**. The League did not possess a standing army and depended too much on the goodwill of its members. It succeeded in solving several disputes between small states in the 1920s, but the big tests for it came in the 1930s.

Study tip

The organisation of the League could be part of a 'describe' question in the exam or a bullet point concerned with the weaknesses or failure of the League. Make sure you know the differences between the parts of the League and its weaknesses in 1920.

Tasks

1 What does Source **A** tell you about the beginning of the League of Nations?

2 Why was the League weak when it was started in 1920?

Did you know ??????

The Permanent Court of Justice was located in the Peace Palace in The Hague. Although its activities ended when the Netherlands was occupied by Germany in 1940, it was not officially closed until 1946.

Key terms

Veto: a vote that blocks a decision being put into effect.

The Manchurian Crisis

Events

Japan had been dissatisfied with the peace settlement at the end of the First World War. The population of Japan was increasing and the depression caused by the Wall Street Crash in 1929 had led to a reduction in markets for Japanese goods and increased poverty and unrest in Japan. Many, including the army, thought that the answer would be the expansion of Japan into Manchuria. This would give room for the surplus population and be a sure market for Japanese goods.

Since 1904 Japan had been allowed to have soldiers in Manchuria guarding the South Manchurian railway. In September 1931 the Japanese claimed that there had been an explosion on the railway line at Mukden, which they said was sabotage by the Chinese. There is no certainty that an explosion took place as transport on the railway was not interrupted, but this gave the Japanese army an excuse to invade. The Japanese army quickly defeated the Chinese at Mukden. The action had been taken by the army without the permission of the government, but its success was so popular in Japan that the army was now in control of Japanese policy.

> **Did you know** ??????
>
> The term 'Wall Street Crash' comes from the Wall Street district of New York, which is the financial centre of the USA. The New York Stock Exchange was the biggest stock market in the world.

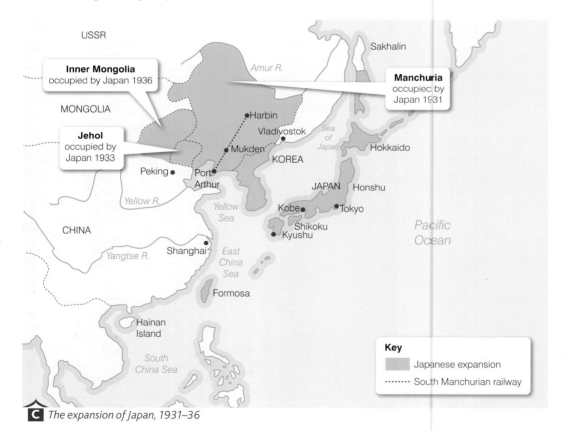

C The expansion of Japan, 1931–36

Action taken by the League

China appealed to the League of Nations and the Lytton Commission was set up by the League to look at the evidence. China claimed that Japan had committed an act of aggression; Japan claimed that it had gone into Manchuria to restore order. The Lytton Commission issued its report a year later. This found that China's rule was chaotic and Japan had some grievances against it, but the Japanese invasion was condemned and it recommended that Manchuria should be a self-governing state. The Japanese then reorganised Manchuria and called it Manchukuo. This was supposed to be an independent state, but it was in fact controlled by Japan. By early 1933 Japan occupied the whole of Manchuria. Later in 1933 the League formally condemned Japan's action. The Japanese simply left the League and later occupied another Chinese province, Jehol.

The effect of the Manchurian Crisis on the League

The League had failed. One of the permanent members of the Council had committed an act of aggression and got away with it. Why did the countries in the League not act?

- Sanctions were discussed but not used because Japan's main trading partner was the USA, which was not in the League, so they would have no effect.
- All the countries were suffering the effects of the economic depression and did not want to be involved with international problems. Britain, in particular, did not want troubles in the Far East to affect its trade in Asia.
- Britain was not prepared to risk its fleet against Japan in the Far East.
- France had no intention of sending troops to the Far East.
- The nearest country to Japan who could send troops was the USSR, but it was not in the League.

No country wanted war against Japan – a stronger Japan was a useful ally against the expansion of the USSR in the Far East. Manchuria was seen as distant from Europe and many regarded the attack as an 'intervention', not an invasion. Japan was restoring order, not invading. At the time it was not considered to be a major blow to the League, but other dissatisfied countries such as Italy and Germany noted the failure and offered later challenges to the League.

Tasks

3 What mistakes did the League make over Manchuria?

4 Study Source **D**.

a Explain the meaning of the cartoon.

b Do you think Source **D** is an accurate view of how the Manchurian Crisis affected the League? Give reasons for your answer.

D 'The Doormat': British cartoon published on 19 January 1933

The Abyssinian Crisis

Background

In 1914 Italy had left the Triple Alliance and refused to go to war as an ally of Germany and Austria-Hungary, eventually entering the war in 1915 as an ally of Britain and France. In spite of finishing the war on the victorious side, Italy had been unhappy with the peace settlement, as it did not receive as much land as the Allies had promised in 1915. This disappointment was partly responsible for the unpopularity of the government after the war and Benito Mussolini had seized power in Italy and set up a fascist dictatorship there.

Mussolini wanted to increase his popularity by restoring the glory of the Roman Empire. Abyssinia (Ethiopia) was one of the few areas of Africa which had not been taken over by European countries. It was next to the Italian colonies of Eritrea and Somaliland, so it would be relatively easy to launch an attack from these areas. The Italians had tried to do this in 1896 but had been defeated at the Battle of Adowa. Mussolini planned to gain revenge for this defeat and the rich pastureland and raw materials of Abyssinia would benefit the Italian economy. A victorious war would divert the Italian people's attention away from the problems caused by the depression of the 1930s and, if Abyssinia became Italian, it would provide a secure market for Italian exports.

Italy, like Japan in 1931, was a permanent member of the Council of the League. The Manchurian Crisis had given Mussolini the impression that the League would not resist an act of aggression by a major power. In 1935 Britain, France and Italy formed a united front against Germany – the Stresa Front – which opposed Germany's aims to change the Treaty of Versailles. The French were so keen to have Italy's support against Hitler that they gave Mussolini the impression that they would not oppose him in Abyssinia.

Study tip

Mussolini is not named in the specification so you will not get a question on his aims, etc. What *is* important for the exam is why the League of Nations was unable to stop him gaining Abyssinia.

Did you know ??????

The Stresa Front agreement was made in the town of Stresa, Italy, between French Foreign Minister Pierre Laval, British Prime Minister Ramsay MacDonald and Mussolini on 14 April 1935.

Key
- → Italian advance
- Italian territory
- French territory
- British territory or strong British influence

E *North-east Africa, 1935–36*

Events

In December 1934 a clash occurred between Italian and Abyssinian soldiers at Wal-Wal on the border between Abyssinia and Italian Somaliland in Africa, with some loss of life. The dispute went to the League for a decision, but it was clear that Mussolini was planning war as the Italians built up their forces in Italian Somaliland on the Abyssinian border. The Peace Ballot of 1935 in Britain showed clearly that the people of Britain believed that support for the League of Nations would keep peace. The British Foreign Secretary, Sir Samuel Hoare, made a speech (Source **G**), which made it appear that Britain would support the idea of collective security in the event of any act of aggression. In spite of all this, Italian forces invaded Abyssinia on 3 October 1935 – Mussolini claiming that he was trying to bring civilisation to Abyssinia.

THE AWFUL WARNING.

FRANCE AND ENGLAND
(together ?).

"WE DON'T WANT YOU TO FIGHT,
BUT, BY JINGO, IF YOU DO,
WE SHALL PROBABLY ISSUE A JOINT MEMORANDUM
SUGGESTING A MILD DISAPPROVAL OF YOU."

F *Cartoon published in a British magazine, 14 August 1935*

Did you know ??????

The Peace Ballot of 1935 was a nationwide questionnaire of five questions to discover the British public's attitude to the League of Nations and collective security. Approximately 11 million people voted.

❝ *If the League succeeds it is because its members have in combination with each other, the will and the power to apply the principles of the Covenant. On behalf of his Majesty's Government in the United Kingdom I can say that they will be second to none in their intention to fulfil the obligations which the Covenant lays upon them.* ❞

G *Speech by Sir Samuel Hoare to the Assembly of the League of Nations, 11 September 1935*

Did you know ??????

By 1936, after the invasion of Abyssinia, Mussolini's official title was 'His Excellency Benito Mussolini, Head of Government, Duce of Fascism, and Founder of the Empire'.

Task

5 Study Sources **F** and **G**.

a What is Source **F** suggesting about how Britain and France were dealing with the Abyssinian Crisis?

b What is Sir Samuel Hoare suggesting in Source **G**?

c How far do you think the two sources are accurate? Explain your answer.

Action taken by the League

Sanctions

Mussolini's invasion was a clear example of an act of aggression committed by a large country against a smaller one. Under the League's rules, action would have to been taken. Moreover, Italy and Abyssinia were relatively close to the main countries in the League, not on the other side of the world like Manchuria and Japan, so action could have been taken and could have been effective. Much to the surprise of Mussolini, the League condemned Italy's invasion as an act of aggression.

In order to work, sanctions needed to be introduced at once. Although trade in arms to Italy was ended immediately and imports from Italy banned, it took over two months for the League to make a decision on other sanctions. Britain and France did not want to lose Mussolini's alliance against Hitler, so they did not want to upset him over Abyssinia. In the end, limited sanctions were placed on Italy. Vital goods that Mussolini needed for the invasion such as oil, coal, iron and steel were excluded from the sanctions. The USA supplied oil to Italy, France continued to provide iron and steel and Britain was afraid that if coal was included it would lead to increased unemployment in the

H *An artist's impression of fighting in Abyssinia showing an Italian attack*

∞ links

The Covenant of the League is covered on page 36.
See pages 38–39 for the Manchurian Crisis.

Did you know ??????

The Italian Empire in Africa also included Eritrea, Italian Somaliland and Libya.

Did you know ??????

The Suez Canal is in Egypt. It allows water to travel between Asia and Europe without having to navigate around Africa. The modern canal opened in 1869, but the remains of several ancient Egyptian canals have been found in this region.

British coal industry. Britain and France could have stopped Italy by closing the Suez Canal to Italian ships – their easiest route to Abyssinia – but they did not want to lose Mussolini's friendship. The refusal to ban trade in iron, steel and coal, together with the failure to close the Suez Canal, are clear examples of Britain and France putting their own selfish interests before those of the League. This was not the 'collective security' expected by Wilson when he had set up the League in 1919.

Hoare–Laval Pact

The Italians fought with tanks, aeroplanes and poison gas against the Abyssinians with their spears and out-of-date rifles. In spite of this, the occupation was not as swift as Mussolini had hoped. In December 1935 Sir Samuel Hoare and the French Prime Minister, Pierre Laval, drafted a secret agreement to solve the crisis. The Hoare–Laval **Pact** gave Italy two thirds of Abyssinia. Mussolini may have accepted this, but when news of this agreement leaked out it was so unpopular in Britain that it had to be dropped and Hoare was forced to resign. In May 1936 the Italians captured Addis Ababa, the capital of Abyssinia. In June, the Emperor of Abyssinia, Haile Selassie, made a personal appeal for further help to the League, but the war was over. Mussolini claimed a great victory and Abyssinia became part of the Italian Empire.

> **Key terms**
>
> **Pact:** an agreement between countries.

The effect of the Abyssinian Crisis on the League

Italy walked out of the League in May 1936 and sanctions were withdrawn in July. The Abyssinian Crisis marked the end of the League as a means of keeping the peace. Of the Great Powers, only Britain, France and the USSR remained in the League. Other means had to be found to prevent war.

> **Did you know** ???????
>
> The term 'axis' was first used by Mussolini. He said that Italy and Germany would form an axis around which the other states of Europe would revolve.

> 66 *There was a very good reason for the League to enforce the particular sanctions they chose, because with an incomplete membership they were the only ones they could impose and which by their own action alone they could hope to see effective. Oil could not be made effective by League action alone.*
>
> *I think it is right that the League should admit that sanctions have not realised their purpose and should face that fact.* 99

I A speech by Anthony Eden, who became British Foreign Secretary after the resignation of Sir Samuel Hoare, explaining to parliament why sanctions should be ended, 18 June 1936

> **links**
>
> For more on the remilitarisation of the Rhineland see page 50.

Hitler had taken advantage of the Abyssinian Crisis when he had reversed the Treaty of Versailles by sending troops into the Rhineland in March 1936, judging correctly that Britain and France would be too occupied by the events in Abyssinia to oppose him. The crisis also ended the Stresa Front. In 1936 Mussolini signed the Rome–Berlin Axis with Hitler, which ended the hopes of France and Britain to keep him as an ally against Germany. In 1937 this was extended when Japan joined the Axis and it became the Anti-Comintern Pact. Italy formally withdrew from the League of Nations in 1937. Europe was clearly dividing into two opposing sides.

> **Did you know** ???????
>
> The Anti-Comintern Pact was specifically directed against the Communist International, known as the Comintern.

Tasks

6   How useful is Source **H** to an historian writing about the events of the Abyssinian Crisis?

7   Read Source **I**.

a   Do you agree with the explanation given by Anthony Eden in Source **I** for the sanctions policy used by the League of Nations against Italy? Explain your answer by referring to other reasons for the failure to impose full sanctions on Italy.

b   Why do you think Eden made this statement in June 1936? What was he hoping to achieve by it?

Hint

Remember to use your own knowledge to develop what you see in each source and to point out what they show. Comment on the provenance of each source and try to work out why it was produced and for whom it was intended (the audience).

Activity

This activity could be completed as a discussion, debate or revision exercise. It requires you to consider the whole of the chapter.

1   Find examples of when and how each of the following contributed to the failure of the League.

a   Membership of the League: the absence of the USA, exclusions, defections of major powers.

b   Lack of full support given by France and Britain.

c   Lack of power to enforce decisions: weakness of moral persuasion, economic sanctions, lack of army.

d   The unfairness of the Treaty of Versailles, which the League had to uphold.

e   Countries were more interested in their own good rather than the international situation, so acted out of self-interest.

f   The depression of the 1930s made countries even more inward-looking and competitive rather than working for the good of all.

g   Decisions took too long.

h   The Manchurian Crisis.

i   The Abyssinian Crisis.

Hint

For Task 7a, don't forget to give a balanced answer – that is, use your own knowledge and look at the provenance of the source to explain how you agree and disagree with the source.

Study tip

'Which of the following two reasons was more important for the failure of the League of Nations?' This is a key question that is likely to come up often in the exam. It is important that you are able to explain and assess the contribution of each factor.

Practice questions

Study **Source A** and then answer all three questions that follow.

Source A   Friedrich Ebert, President of Germany in 1920, comments on the Treaty of Versailles

> We shall never forget those Germans who are to be severed from us. They will be torn from the Reich [Empire], but they will not be torn from our hearts.

1   The main decisions at Versailles were taken by the leaders of the three greatest countries that attended: Clemenceau for France, Lloyd George for Britain and Wilson for the USA. Describe the aims of these 'Big Three'.   *(4 marks)*

2   **Source A** suggests one reason why Germany objected to the land it lost at Versailles.

    Do you agree that this was the main reason for German opposition to the territorial terms of the treaty?

    Explain your answer by referring to the purpose of the source as well as using its content and your knowledge.   *(6 marks)*

3   Which was the more important reason for the weakness of the League of Nations:

- the membership of the League from 1919 to 1939;
- the organisation and peacekeeping powers of the League of Nations?

    You must refer to **both** reasons when explaining your answer.   *(10 marks)*

3.1 How did Hitler challenge and exploit the Treaty of Versailles from 1933 to March 1938?

A *Hitler playing with all the statesmen of Europe*

Objectives

In this chapter you will learn about:

Hitler's aims in foreign policy

the methods used by Hitler to change the Treaty of Versailles

the policy of appeasement

the events leading up to the outbreak of war in 1939

whether the war could have been avoided

who or what caused the Second World War.

Hitler's aims in foreign policy

While in prison in 1924, Hitler wrote *Mein Kampf* ('My Struggle'). In this and later writings in the 1920s, he made some comments about his aims in foreign policy. His main aims can be summarised as follows:

- to make Germany into a Great Power again
- to unite all German speaking people under his rule
- to gain territory for Germany in the East to provide *Lebensraum* ('living space') for the German people.

Achieving Hitler's aims

To achieve these aims, it would be necessary to destroy the Treaty of Versailles. Hitler had gained much support in Germany throughout the 1920s by condemning the treaty and the politicians who had signed it. He blamed many of Germany's problems on the peace settlement. The treaty was a symbol of Germany's defeat and the disgrace that came with it. When Hitler came to power, reparations had been reduced and eventually cancelled in 1932. The remainder of the hated treaty remained in force, so in order to further his aims Hitler would have to:

- change the territorial settlement of the Treaty of Versailles by regaining lands inhabited by German people that had been taken from Germany at Versailles, including the Saar and Danzig

Study tip

This topic overlaps with the previous chapter. You can only understand Hitler's foreign policy if you are aware of the Treaty of Versailles and the failure of the League of Nations.

∞ links

For more detail on the territorial settlement of Versailles, see pages 31–32.

- bring the 7 million German-speaking people in Austria, and the 4 million in Czechoslovakia and Poland, into his empire – this again involved destroying the peace settlement of 1919

- build up the German army so that his aims could be supported by force if necessary and to prove that Germany was a Great Power

- expand in the east, probably against communist USSR – Hitler hated Communism. This aim was probably intended for the future when the Treaty of Versailles had been overturned and Germany confirmed as the greatest power in Europe.

The first stage of Germany's struggle would be to strengthen its lands in Europe. This could not be done alone. Hitler felt that the main enemies of Germany were France and the USSR, so he aimed to get the friendship of Italy and Britain against them.

Did you know ??????

Hitler hated Communism because he was a nationalist. He loved his country more than anything, whereas communists were devoted to a cause that went beyond national boundaries. Their country was not as important to them.

> " *It was necessary for us [the Nazi Party] to dig ourselves into the minds of the people as the enemies of the peace treaties so that the people will give us their confidence.* "

B *Hitler's use of the Treaty of Versailles. From* Mein Kampf *by Adolf Hitler*

Tasks

1 What is the message of Source **A**?

2 Which of Hitler's aims was the most likely to involve him in dispute with Britain and France?

3 Which countries do you think he wanted to take over? Use Source **H** on page 31 to help you.

4 What did Hitler mean by Source **B**? Which parts of the Treaty of Versailles do you think he would use to gain support?

5 Look back at the Treaty of Versailles on pages 30–35.

a Which parts of the treaty do you think Hitler would try to reverse first? Give reasons for your answer.

b Try to plan the order in which you would expect Hitler to try to change the treaty. As you go through the chapter, check your order and see how far Hitler kept to what you expected.

Timeline

Hitler's foreign policy and the outbreak of war

	1933	Germany withdraws from the League of Nations
Jan	1934	Hitler signs 10-year non-aggression pact with Poland
Jul	1934	Mussolini prevents Anschluss
Jan	1935	Saar returned to Germany
Apr	1935	Stresa Front formed
Jun	1935	Anglo-German Naval Agreement
Oct	1935	Mussolini invades Abyssinia
Mar	1936	Rhineland remilitarised
Oct	1936	Rome–Berlin Axis signed
	1936–39	Spanish Civil War
May	1937	Chamberlain becomes British Prime Minister; his policy of appeasement begins
Mar	1938	Anschluss
Sep	1938	Munich Conference
Mar	1939	Collapse of Czechoslovakia
Aug	1939	Nazi–Soviet Pact
Sep	1939	Attack on Poland and outbreak of the Second World War

German rearmament

C *Roll call of German troops in Nuremberg, 1935*

Task

6 Study Source **C**.

a Why was this photo published in Germany in 1935?

b Explain what you can learn about Hitler and Germany in 1935 from this source.

Study tip

Take note of the methods used by Hitler – how he managed to divert the other powers with his promises. See how he uses this method later.

Germany was allowed to join the League of Nations in 1926. One of the aims of the League had been to maintain peace by reducing the arms of all countries, but it had achieved little success by 1932 when the Disarmament Conference began. As a member of the League, Germany was allowed to attend the conference. It soon became obvious that France would never disarm because of its fears of another German attack. In 1933 Hitler withdrew Germany from the Disarmament Conference and from the League of Nations. He insisted that Germany wanted peace and would be prepared to disarm if other countries did. Germany began to rearm, introducing conscription in 1935. Hitler's excuse was that France had just increased its term of conscription from 12 to 18 months, which would increase the number of trained soldiers in France.

The rearmament of Germany was clearly against the Treaty of Versailles, so why did Britain and France not act? The only opposition was the formation of the short-lived Stresa Front to protest against the introduction of conscription in Germany. Also, Soviet Russia, afraid of a strong Germany, joined the League of Nations. Many in Britain felt that the Treaty of Versailles was unfair and needed to be revised. On the other hand, the French were afraid of German recovery and wanted to see the Treaty strengthened, not weakened, but could not act alone. In any case, what could they do? Invade Germany? They had tried this in 1923 when they had occupied the Ruhr because Germany had fallen behind in reparations payments, but this method had failed. Differences between Britain and France had begun to emerge then and Britain had sympathised with Germany not France.

Hitler took advantage of these differences between Britain and France to further his aims in foreign policy. Although he often threatened to use force to achieve his aims, every time he acted against the treaty he followed it with promises of peace. Britain paid more attention to these promises than to the reversal of the treaty.

Ten-year non-aggression pact

In 1934 Hitler signed a *Ten-year non-aggression pact with Poland*, which guaranteed the boundaries of Poland. This satisfied the Poles that Hitler would not try to take back the Polish Corridor. It pleased Britain, who saw it as further proof that Hitler's aims were peaceful, as it meant that Germany had accepted the frontier with Poland set up at Versailles.

Failed Anschluss

Later in 1934 Hitler suffered a setback to his aims. He encouraged the Austrian Nazi Party to rebel and this resulted in the murder of the Austrian Chancellor, Dollfuss. It looked as if Hitler's aim of the reunification of Germany and Austria (*Anschluss*) was going to be achieved. It was prevented by Mussolini moving his army to the frontier of Austria and guaranteeing Austrian independence. Hitler realised that his army was not strong enough, so he backed down and denied any involvement with the Austrian Nazi Party.

Anglo-German Naval Agreement and rearmament

More successful for Hitler was the signing of the *Anglo-German Naval Agreement* in 1935. Hitler's willingness to sign it was further proof to Britain of his peaceful intentions. The treaty limited the German navy to 35 per cent of the strength of the British fleet, but did not include submarines. By signing this agreement, Britain had agreed to Germany rearming. Clearly, Britain felt that if there was to be no agreement on disarmament, then it was important for Britain to limit the size of the German navy. It was a success for Hitler because the agreement weakened the Stresa Front as Britain had not consulted France and Italy, and it led to Germany proceeding with rearmament without opposition. By 1938 the German army had reached around 800,000, the navy had 47 **U-boats** and the air force had over 2,000 aircraft.

links

See page 43 for the Stresa Front.

Tasks

7   What opposition was there to Hitler rearming? Explain clearly how his methods dealt with this opposition.

8   What can you learn about Hitler from the events in Austria in 1934? What lesson does this appear to give about opposing him?

9   Why do you think Hitler made the non-aggression pact with Poland and the Naval Agreement with Britain?

Did you know ??????

In forming the non-aggression pact with Poland, Hitler broke with tradition. Relations between Germany and Poland had never been particularly good. The pact was probably meant to keep up the appearance of non-aggression and buy Germany time for rearmament.

Did you know ??????

For Britain, the Anglo-German Naval Agreement was mainly a way of measuring German intentions towards it, and possibly a move towards further treaties to protect Britain. Hitler was disappointed when it did not lead to an alliance between the two countries.

Key terms

U-boat: German name for a submarine, short for *Unterseeboot* (*U-Boot*).

The return of the Saar

In January 1935 a plebiscite was held in the Saar to decide whether it should remain under the control of the League of Nations, return to German control or join France. The Saar was inhabited by mainly German people, so the result was never in any doubt. Around 90 per cent voted to rejoin Germany, 8 per cent wanted to remain under the control of the League and 2 per cent wanted to join France. Nazi propaganda made great use of this. Victory in the plebiscite was publicised as the removal of one of the injustices of Versailles. It was greeted with great celebration in Germany. Hitler announced to the world that all cause of grievance between France and Germany had now been removed. The return of the Saar to Germany was not illegal. Hitler had kept within the terms of the Treaty of Versailles, which had provided for a plebiscite to be held after 15 years.

The remilitarisation of the Rhineland

Events

On 7 March 1936 German soldiers marched into the Rhineland. This was against the Treaty of Versailles and the Locarno Pact, which the German government had willingly signed in 1925. Hitler followed up the remilitarisation with promises that Germany would sign a 25-year non-aggression pact and had no further territorial ambitions in Europe. Britain, France and the League of Nations should have acted against Germany. All that happened was that German action was condemned by the League but, when a vote was cast, only Soviet Russia voted in favour of imposing sanctions on Germany.

E *German troops in the Rhineland, March 1936*

⬤⬤ links

See pages 30–33 for the terms of the Treaty of Versailles.

D *A stamp issued in Germany to commemorate the return of the Saar*

Hint

In explaining the reaction of the German people to the soldiers in Source **E**, use your knowledge to support or oppose this. How would this have affected foreign opposition? Try to explain why this photo was taken.

Tasks

10   Explain how the beginning of rearmament differed from the return of the Saar in 1935.

11   Explain what Source **D** tells you about the importance of the Saar to Germany.

12   How useful is Source **E** to an historian writing about the remilitarisation of the Rhineland?

Why was there no action against Hitler?

Hitler had chosen his moment carefully. Britain and France were more concerned about Mussolini's invasion of Abyssinia. The French government was divided and not prepared to act without the support of Britain. Britain felt that Hitler was doing nothing wrong. The Treaty of Versailles was unjust and therefore Hitler was right to change it. Germany was only moving troops into its own territory. It was not like Mussolini, who had invaded another country. No one wanted war and people took far more notice of Hitler's promises. At the end of March, Hitler held a vote in Germany on his policies: 99 per cent of those who voted were in favour of them.

Did you know ??????

When German troops entered the Rhineland, many of them rode on bicycles.

Did you know ??????

The vote after the remilitarisation of the Rhineland was used to demonstrate German support for Hitler's government. Hitler knew the remilitarisation was one of his most popular actions and cleverly used it as propaganda to the rest of the world.

∞ **links**

See page 32 for more on the Rhineland in the Treaty of Versailles.

See pages 40–43 for the Abyssinian Crisis.

THE GOOSE-STEP

"GOOSEY GOOSEY GANDER,
WHITHER DOST THOU WANDER?"
"ONLY THROUGH THE RHINELAND—
PRAY EXCUSE MY BLUNDER!"

F *British cartoon on the Rhineland, 18 March 1936. The goose step is a method of marching used by the Nazi army*

Task

13 Sources **F** and **G** are both British. Explain how they disagree. Why do you think they have different ideas? How far do you think they are accurate views of the remilitarisation of the Rhineland?

❝ *Germany was only 'going into her own back garden'.* ❞

G *Statement by Lord Lothian, a British politician describing the remilitarisation*

Could Hitler have been stopped in 1936?

There is no doubt that Hitler took a chance when he sent soldiers into the Rhineland. He did it against the advice of his generals who considered that the army was not strong enough to resist if the French army opposed them. It was also against the advice of his financial ministers who feared the effect that economic sanctions could have had on Germany. Hitler took all these considerations into account but dismissed them. His generals had orders that, if there was any opposition from the French, Germany would withdraw immediately.

All the fears of Hitler's ministers were justified. The French army was far stronger than that of Germany in 1936 and sanctions would have crippled Germany, but Hitler had judged foreign reactions perfectly. Germany could have been stopped, but there was no support for opposition. If the French army had invaded the Rhineland, perhaps Hitler would have become more popular in Germany as the victim of foreign invasion. Britain was satisfied that Germany was justified and another grievance of the Treaty of Versailles had been eliminated. Once all of these grievances had been dealt with, Germany would be satisfied and live in peace with other nations. Hitler could have been stopped, but the will to use force against him was not there.

Results of remilitarisation

The Rhineland had a decisive effect on later events:

- Hitler had successfully reversed the Treaty of Versailles, giving him the confidence to go further. The main remaining territorial grievance of Versailles was Danzig and the Polish Corridor.
- The position of Hitler in Germany had been strengthened: he had been proved to be right and his army and ministers wrong. In spite of opposition from his ministers, his nerve had held and he had been successful. Again, this increased his confidence.
- It led to the signing of the Rome–Berlin Axis with Mussolini. Italy and Germany were to cooperate in their support for the fascist General Franco in the Spanish Civil War of 1936–39. This gave Hitler an opportunity to test his armed forces, weapons and tactics and gave both German and Italian troops experience of war.
- The remilitarisation of the Rhineland followed by the signing of the Rome–Berlin Axis meant the end of the attempts of Britain and France to keep Mussolini as an ally against Hitler. Both countries had shown their unwillingness to oppose the aggression of the dictators.
- There was some movement towards rearmament in Britain.
- French security was not affected because the French had begun the building of the Maginot Line, a vast series of fortifications on the border between France and Germany.
- Together with the Abyssinian Crisis, it marked the end of the League of Nations as a means of keeping peace.

Did you know ??????

Adolf Hitler never visited Britain.

Task

14 What were the differences between the occupation of the Saar and the remilitarisation of the Rhineland? Explain your answer.

Did you know ??????

The Spanish Civil War was a war between republicans and fascists, which divided European opinion. It caused hostility between communist USSR and the Axis powers. Both provided assistance – men and weapons – to the opposing sides.

Study tip

If you are asked to assess the part played by the Rhineland in the start of the Second World War, it is not sufficient to give just the results; you must illustrate them with reference to what happened later.

> ❝ *The forty-eight hours after the march into the Rhineland were the most nerve-racking in my life. If the French had then marched into the Rhineland we would have had to withdraw in disgrace, for the military resources at our disposal would have been inadequate for even a modest resistance.* ❞

 H *Hitler speaking later about the remilitarisation*

Task

16 Look back at Hitler's aims on page 46.

  a Draw a table with three columns, one headed **Hitler's aims**, the second **Month and year he achieved them (When)** and the third **How he achieved them (How)**. Use the information in this chapter to complete the table up to 1936.

  b Use your table to work out which of Hitler's aims he had been most successful in achieving by the end of 1936. Explain your answer.

  c Using his aims, what do you think Hitler would attempt to achieve next? Explain why.

  d When you have finished this chapter, complete your table up to September 1939.

  e Some historians believe that Hitler had a plan in foreign policy that he carried out in the 1930s, others believe that he just took advantage of the opportunities presented to him. Does your table show any pattern to his aims?

Task

15 Read Source **H**.

  a How does this source help you to understand Hitler's methods in foreign policy?

  b What did Hitler gain from the remilitarisation?

  c Do you think the remilitarisation was an opportunity to stop him? Explain your answer.

▮ Anschluss with Austria

The union of Austria and Germany (Anschluss) had been forbidden by the Treaty of Versailles. Hitler was born within the boundaries of Austria and had stated in *Mein Kampf* that he felt the rightful place of Austria was in a union with Germany. In 1934 the Austrian Nazis, encouraged by Hitler, had tried to seize power after the murder of the Austrian Chancellor, Dollfuss. This had been prevented by Mussolini who had been prepared to give support to Austria. By 1938, the situation had changed: Mussolini was now allied with Germany and occupied in the Spanish Civil War, so he was unlikely to give help to Austria. One of Hitler's aims was to unite all German-speaking people under his leadership, and the Austrians were German-speaking.

The Nazi Party remained strong in Austria and early in 1938 there were rumours of another Nazi plot to overthrow the Austrian government. The Austrian Chancellor, Schuschnigg, appealed to Hitler for help to end the plotting. Hitler refused and, instead of helping, he put pressure on Schuschnigg and forced him to appoint Seyss-Inquart, the leader of the Nazi Party in Austria, as Minister of the Interior, in charge of the police force. This was followed by a series of riots and demonstrations by the Nazis in Austria, encouraged by Hitler. In spite of his position, Seyss-Inquart supported the demonstrations and did nothing to stop them.

∞ links

For more information on the failed Anschluss, see page 49.

Did you know ??????

German troops entering Austria were greeted by German flags and flowers – the invasion is often known as the *Blumenkrieg* ('war of flowers') – and 200,000 Austrians gathered in the *Heldenplatz* ('Square of Heroes') in Vienna to welcome Hitler.

I *Hitler parades through Vienna, March 1938*

Schuschnigg made a bold move to end the disturbances and to try and save the independence of Austria. He called a plebiscite on whether the Austrian people wanted to remain independent or not. This alarmed Hitler. There were many Austrians who favoured Anschluss because they felt that the Austrian economy was too weak to remain independent, but Hitler was not prepared to take the risk.

It was clear to everyone that Schuschnigg had defied Hitler by calling the plebiscite without his permission and he could not afford anything other than an overwhelming vote in favour of unification with Germany. To make certain that he got this and kept in control, Hitler moved German troops to the border and forced Schuschnigg to call off the plebiscite and resign from office. All through the crisis, Schuschnigg had probably expected Britain and France to give assistance to Austria. When it was clear that this was not going to happen and wanting to avoid bloodshed, Schuschnigg resigned.

Did you know ? ? ? ? ?

The West End musical *The Sound of Music* is set at the time of the Anschluss and features a family who escaped from the Nazi takeover.

⊕ **links**

For Wilson's fourteen points, turn back to page 29.

Seyss-Inquart replaced Schuschnigg as Chancellor and invited the Germans into Austria to restore order. The German army entered on 12 March. First of all, opponents of Hitler were eliminated. Around 80,000 were rounded up and placed in concentration camps. Seyss-Inquart handed over power to Hitler and Anschluss was proclaimed. On 14 March Hitler processed in triumph through Vienna. This was followed by a plebiscite in April in which 99.75 per cent of voters agreed to the Anschluss. Hitler could claim that he was only fulfilling the idea of self-determination expressed in Woodrow Wilson's Fourteen Points.

Britain and France protested but did nothing; the League of Nations was not consulted. Although Anschluss was against the Treaty of Versailles, Britain had sympathy with Germany because the Austrians were German-speaking and German in tradition and culture; moreover, the Austrians had shown what they wanted in the plebiscite. The British government also feared Communism in the USSR more than it did Nazism and welcomed a strong Germany because it saw it as a barrier to the USSR and Communism. Hitler's anti-communist beliefs strengthened this view.

Results of Anschluss

- A triumph for Germany – Hitler now had the resources of Austria at his disposal. This included the army as well as economic resources of iron and steel.
- Another 'injustice' to Germany of the Treaty of Versailles had been overcome without opposition. Hitler's confidence continued to grow.
- Germany now possessed land on three sides of the western part of Czechoslovakia – the Sudetenland – which was inhabited by over 3 million German-speaking people.
- It proved the value of Hitler's alliance with Mussolini.
- Anschluss was not unpopular in Austria. Although the plebiscite results were exaggerated by the Nazi presence, many Austrians welcomed being joined to the glory of the new Germany.

> 66 *Over ten million Germans live in two states next to Germany. It is in the interest of the German Reich [Empire] to protect them.* 99

J *Hitler speaking in February 1938*

Did you know ??????

Austria became known as the province of Ostmark after the Anschluss. Seyss-Inquart drafted the legislative act reducing Austria to a province of Germany and signed it into law on 13 March.

Study tip

If you are asked to assess the part played by the Anschluss in the start of the Second World War, you must develop the points here and link them to the events that occurred afterwards.

Tasks

17 How useful is Source I to an historian studying the popularity of the Anschluss?

18 How many of Hitler's aims did achieving the Anschluss fulfil?

19 Study Source J.
  a   Which countries was Hitler referring to in Source J?
  b   What justification is there for Hitler's statement?

20 Why did Anschluss succeed in 1938 when it had failed in 1934?

21 What impression would the reaction of the powers to the remilitarisation and to the Anschluss give to Hitler? How might it affect his future policies?

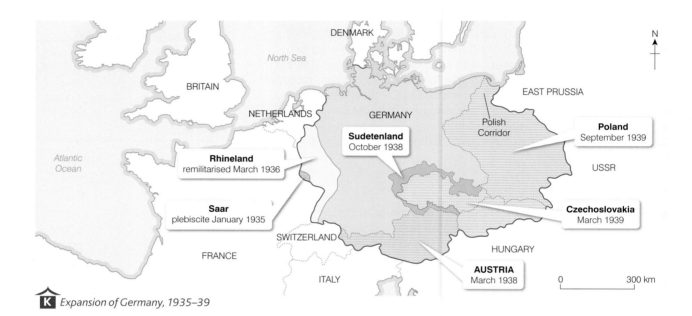

K *Expansion of Germany, 1935–39*

Tasks

22 Use the map to work out which new frontiers Germany gained by the Anschluss.

23 Did the Anschluss strengthen Germany? Give reasons for your answer.

24 Which country looked to be in the greatest danger from Germany after the Anschluss?

25 Did Hitler have a legitimate reason for attacking this country? Explain what it was.

3.2 Why did Chamberlain's policy of appeasement fail to prevent the outbreak of war in 1939?

▣ Appeasement

Appeasement is the name often given to British foreign policy in the years 1919 to 1939, but it is particularly associated with Neville Chamberlain who became Prime Minister in 1937. Chamberlain believed in taking an active role in solving Hitler's grievances. He felt that Germany had good reason to be upset at many of the terms of the Treaty of Versailles. What he wanted to do was to find out exactly what Hitler wanted and show him that reasonable claims could be met by negotiation instead of by force. In this way, the problems of Versailles would be solved, Germany would be satisfied and there would be no war. Chamberlain was aware of the risks of appeasement.

The risks were that it depended on Hitler's aims being reasonable and limited to righting the wrongs of the Treaty of Versailles. It meant trusting Hitler and believing that he was telling the truth. After 1937 France supported appeasement because of the increased security it had with the building of the Maginot Line. Chamberlain's first test was the Anschluss, which was accepted by Britain because it was seen as taking over a German-speaking area.

> ❝ *What country in Europe today, if threatened by a large power, can rely on the League of Nations for protection? None.* ❞

A *Chamberlain speaking in the House of Commons, 7 March 1938*

Arguments in favour of appeasement

- The feeling that Germany had genuine grievances that could be solved.
- People in Britain wanted to avoid another war at all costs. They remembered the loss of life in the First World War and the Spanish Civil War showed that any future war could be even more horrific, as had been shown at **Guernica**.
- Economically, Britain was still suffering from the depression and could not afford any rearmament programme.
- The collapse of the League of Nations meant that something else had to be tried to keep peace. Chamberlain believed that his idea of personal diplomacy would work.
- Many people in Britain feared communist USSR more than Hitler's fascism and welcomed the recovery of Germany as a barrier between Soviet Russia and the West.

∞ links

See pages 53–55 for the Anschluss.

Key profile

Neville Chamberlain

1869	Born 18 March; educated at Rugby School
1915	Becomes Mayor of Birmingham
1918	Elected to parliament to represent Birmingham Ladywood
1923	Appointed to the office of Postmaster General
1924	Becomes Minister of Health
1931	Appointed Chancellor of the Exchequer
1937	Elected Prime Minister
1939	Declares war on Germany
1940	Resigns as Prime Minister (replaced by Churchill); dies 8 November

Key terms

Guernica: an undefended town in Spain that was bombed for three hours by the Germans in 1937, resulting in 2,500 casualties.

Task

1 What reason was Chamberlain giving in Source **A** for his policy of appeasement?

Arguments against appeasement

- It could not possibly work because Hitler could not be trusted as he had already broken many promises since 1933.
- Appeasement made Britain look weak and gave Hitler the confidence and belief that he would never be opposed by Britain.
- It could be seen as betraying lands that had been protected by the Treaty of Versailles.
- It allowed Hitler to increase his strength and power.

Chamberlain was one of the ministers who had pushed for increased rearmament in Britain after the remilitarisation of the Rhineland, but appeasement did become a personal crusade.

Study tip

Chamberlain's policy of appeasement began with Anschluss. It did not include the Rhineland.

Hint

For Task 2b, check the date Hitler said each source and the different audiences for them.

> 66 *Rauschning: Do you seriously intend to fight the West?*
>
> *Hitler: What else do you think we're arming for? We must proceed step by step, so that no one will interfere with our advance. How to do this I don't yet know. But that it will be done is guaranteed by Britain's lack of firmness and France's internal disunity.* 99

B *A conversation between Rauschning and Hitler in 1934. Rauschning spent much time with Hitler in between 1932 and 1934*

> 66 *It should be possible to end this useless conflict between Germany and France which has lasted for centuries. Why not replace it with the rule of reason? The German people have no interest in seeing the French people suffer. And what advantage can come to France when Germany is in misery?* 99

C *Hitler's speech to the German parliament, 7 March 1936*

■ The Sudetenland Crisis

A chance for Chamberlain to put his ideas of appeasement into practice came with the crisis in the Sudetenland in 1938. The Sudetenland is the western part of Czechoslovakia. It was inhabited by more than 3 million German-speaking people. After the Anschluss, Hitler wanted to take over Czechoslovakia and the Sudeten Germans were the excuse. Czechoslovakia was one of the strongest of the new states created by the treaties of 1919. It had strong, well-fortified frontiers especially in the west. Hitler encouraged Henlein, the leader of the Nazis in the Sudetenland, to campaign for independence and riots broke out. Hitler promised Henlein that he could depend on the support of Germany. Chamberlain was determined to use appeasement to prevent war breaking out over Czechoslovakia.

On 15 September 1938, Chamberlain flew to Germany to find out what Hitler wanted and met him at Berchtesgaden. There Hitler told Chamberlain that he wanted all the German-speaking parts of the Sudetenland to join Germany, but only after plebiscites. Chamberlain then got the support of France for this and Britain and France forced President Benes of Czechoslovakia to accept the deal. Benes realised that he could not depend on the support of Britain and France if Hitler invaded; only Soviet Russia promised to help Czechoslovakia.

Task

2 Read Sources **B** and **C**.

a Sources **B** and **C** are both by Hitler, yet they are different. How are they different?

b Why do you think they give different ideas?

c Which of the two sources would give some hope for appeasement? Explain why by referring to both sources.

Did you know ??????

In 1939, Henlein was named *Gauleiter* (regional leader) of the Sudetenland. He held the position until the end of the war.

Did you know ??????

The Sudetenland was part of Austria-Hungary in 1914, not Germany.

Chamberlain then returned to Germany and, on 22 September, met Hitler at Godesberg. Hitler was taken by surprise; he did not expect Chamberlain to persuade France and Czechoslovakia to accept his demands. So he asked for more: the immediate occupation of the Sudetenland by Germany. There would be no plebiscites. Chamberlain, disappointed, returned to London and Britain prepared for war. In London, preparations were made for defence against air raids: trenches were dug, children evacuated and gas masks given out. It was at this moment that Chamberlain received a note from Hitler inviting him to a conference of four powers to be held in Munich.

> 66 *How horrible, fantastic, incredible it is that we should be digging trenches and trying on gas masks here because of a quarrel in a far away country between people of whom we know nothing.* 99

D *Chamberlain's radio broadcast after Godesberg, 27 September*

The Munich Conference and Agreement

Four powers were represented at this conference: Chamberlain and Hitler, Mussolini for Italy and Daladier for France. No representatives from Czechoslovakia or the USSR were invited. At Munich on 30 September it was agreed that the Sudetenland would become German. Britain and France guaranteed the remaining part of Czechoslovakia. The Czechs were forced to accept this. Chamberlain then met Hitler privately and Hitler agreed to a declaration that Britain and Germany would never go to war again and that consultation not war would solve all future disagreements between them. This is the piece of paper that Chamberlain had in his hand when he returned to Britain on 1 October.

E *Chamberlain on his return to Britain after Munich*

Did you know ??????

The Czech army in 1938 was a considerable force and it was backed up with the Skoda armaments factory, one of the best in Europe.

Did you know ??????

Hitler had always hated the Czechs as he saw them as members of the Slav *Untermenschen* – the sub-humans – and inferior to Germans.

Did you know ??????

Édouard Daladier was the French minister for war. He was far more wary of Hitler's intentions, but allowed Chamberlain to appease Germany under pressure from both Britain and members of the French government and military.

Tasks

3 Explain the meaning of Source **D**.

4 What impression does this source give you of Chamberlain's view of the Czechs?

The importance of the Munich Agreement

- Hitler had gained the Sudetenland without fighting.
- Czechoslovakia had been betrayed.
- Peace had been maintained by Chamberlain.
- Czechoslovakia had lost its defensive frontier and became vulnerable to invasion.
- Germany had gained the armaments and mineral resources of the Sudetenland.
- Britain speeded up rearmament.
- The USSR had been left out and felt betrayed.

Study tip

The Munich Agreement is seen as the great success of appeasement. In the exam you could be asked to describe the Sudeten crisis, to examine the various views on the success or failure of Munich or to assess the part appeasement or Munich played in the outbreak of the Second World War. It is important to assess its success in the light of the events of 1939.

F 'Our new defence', a British cartoon of 5 October 1938

G Results of public opinion polls in Britain, 1938

Date	Question	Result
March 1938	Should Britain promise assistance to Czechoslovakia if Germany acts as it did towards Austria?	Yes: 33% No: 43% Don't know: 24%
October 1938	Hitler says he has no more territorial ambitions in Europe. Do you believe him?	Yes: 7% No: 93%

Task

5 Study Source **F**.

a What can we learn about the Munich Agreement from this source?

b Does it give an accurate view?

> ❝ I will begin by saying the most unpopular and most unwelcome thing, namely that we have sustained a total and unmitigated defeat. I think that in future the Czechoslovak State cannot remain independent. You will find that in a period of time which may be measured by years, but may be measured by only months, Czechoslovakia will be taken over by the Nazi regime. ❞

H Churchill speaking in parliament in the debate on Munich, 5 October 1938

> ❝ If war had come over Czechoslovakia it would have been, as in 1914, to prevent one country from dominating the continent by brutal force. For that principle we must ever be prepared to fight, for on the day when we are not prepared to fight for it we forfeit our liberties and our independence. ❞

I Duff Cooper explains his resignation as First Lord of the Admiralty in protest at the Munich Agreement

> ❝ Applause for Mr Chamberlain. No conqueror returning from a victory on the battlefield had come decorated with nobler laurels. ❞

J Article from The Times on Chamberlain and the Munich Agreement

K German troops entering the Sudetenland

Tasks

6 Discuss the support and opposition that the Munich Agreement had in Britain.

7 Study Sources **F** to **K**.

a Divide the sources into two groups: those that support Munich and those that oppose it. Explain the different views.

b Find other views on the Munich Agreement. Do you think the majority view was in favour or against?

Study tip

Task 8 on page 62 is an examination-style question. To obtain full marks you must say how far you agree with the source and how far you disagree. You must use your knowledge and examine why the historian wrote this. It is not enough to say he was a Soviet and therefore he was biased. Try to look at something he was defending or trying to justify. You will need to consider the events of 1939 to do this.

> ❝ *The governments of Great Britain and France wanted to direct German aggression towards the east, to satisfy Hitler's claims at the expense of the East European countries. They feared the increase of Germany's strength in Europe, but they hoped to appease Hitler by giving him some Czech territory, and counted on involving Germany and Russia in conflict, thus weakening them both.* ❞

L *A Soviet historian writing about the Munich Agreement. From* Anti Soviet Conspiracy *by A. O. Chubaryan, 1969*

■ The collapse of Czechoslovakia

Czechoslovakia had lost 70 per cent of its heavy industry as well as its defensive frontier at Munich. In October 1938 Poland gained the province of Teschen from Czechoslovakia and, in November, Hungary increased its land at the expense of Czechoslovakia. In 1939, encouraged by Hitler, the Slovaks began to press for independence and, in March 1939, the Czech President, Hacha, was forced to hand Czechoslovakia over to Hitler. Hitler marched in, claiming to be restoring order. Most of Czechoslovakia came under German rule. Britain and France protested but did not oppose directly. However, the direction of British foreign policy began to change.

Tasks

8 Source **L** suggests a reason why Chamberlain signed the Munich Agreement with Hitler. Do you agree that this was the main reason? Explain your answer by referring to the purpose of the source, as well as using its content and your own knowledge.

9 Compare Sources **K** and **M**. Explain what we can learn from these two sources about the German takeover of Czechoslovakia.

10 Do you think both sources are accurate? Explain your answer.

M *German troops enter Prague, March 1939*

The effect of Hitler's takeover of Czechoslovakia

- It marked the end of appeasement: Hitler could not justify taking Czechoslovakia. There were no German speakers living there and there was no demand from the people to join Germany. Hitler could not argue that he was reversing the wrongs of the Treaty of Versailles.

- Hitler had proved to Chamberlain that he could not be trusted. Chamberlain felt personally upset with Hitler as he had not only broken the Munich Agreement but had also broken the promise he made personally with Chamberlain to consult Britain before taking action that could lead to war.

- Lithuania was forced to surrender the province of Memel, which had a mostly German population, to Germany. Hitler made it clear that he wanted the restoration of Danzig.

- Britain did not help Czechoslovakia but, supported by France, signed an agreement with Poland promising to help if Poland was invaded.

- Mussolini, Hitler's ally, conquered Albania.

- Britain guaranteed the independence of Romania and Greece.

- Conscription was introduced into Britain during peace time.

- Hitler strengthened his relationship with Mussolini by signing the Pact of Steel.

- Hitler withdrew Germany's non-aggression pact of 1934 with Poland and the Anglo-German Naval Agreement of 1935.

∞ links

For the loss of Danzig, see page 31.

Study tip

March 1939 is often regarded as a turning point in British policy towards Hitler. You should be able to explain why this is so.

∞ links

See page 49 for the Pact with Poland and the Anglo-German Naval Agreement.

■ The role of the USSR

Britain, France and the USSR

In April 1939 Britain and France had guaranteed the frontiers of Poland against any attack. In fact, there was no way that they could have helped Poland if it had been attacked because of the distance away from the West. The only country that could defend Poland against any German attack was the USSR. Britain and France began talks with the Soviets to reach an agreement with them. A major problem for Britain and France was that they knew that Poland was just as afraid of Soviet ambitions as they were of German plans and they did not want help from the Soviet Union. The Poles felt that if a Soviet army entered Poland to defend them against Germany, it would not leave.

Throughout the 1930s the USSR had felt that Britain had been trying to direct Hitler to the East and it is true that there were many in Britain who feared Communism more than Fascism. Evidence of this was the USSR's exclusion from the Munich Conference when clearly the future of Czechoslovakia was important to it. In 1939 Britain and France showed no urgency in making an agreement with the USSR. This made Stalin, the Soviet leader, more suspicious of their aims and led to him signing the Nazi–Soviet Pact with Hitler in August 1939.

Did you know ??????

Not only was there a fear of Communism itself, but many in Britain also believed that the USSR wanted a war between Britain and Germany so that they would destroy one another and leave the USSR as the main European power.

Task

11 Why do you think the USSR thought that Britain did not want to ally with it?

The Nazi–Soviet Pact

This pact came as a surprise. Fascism and Communism were sworn enemies and Hitler's ideas of *Lebensraum* were partly at the expense of the USSR. Hitler had never hidden his opposition to Communism as expressed in *Mein Kampf*. The Nazi–Soviet Pact went against the Anti-Comintern Pact that Hitler had signed with Italy and Japan in 1937, which was opposed to Communism. In the pact, the USSR and Germany agreed not to interfere against the other power in the event of a war. Secret clauses divided Poland between them – the USSR receiving the land it had lost at the end of the First World War and Germany receiving the west of Poland including Danzig and the Polish Corridor. Stalin had gained time to prepare the USSR for the expected attack from Germany.

The importance of the pact

- It meant that Hitler's attack on Poland was inevitable. Hitler had prevented the danger of a war on two fronts, which had been the downfall of Germany in the First World War.
- Hitler presumed it would prevent Britain from opposing his attack on Poland. He thought Britain would back down as it had at Munich, especially as Danzig was clearly German and the Polish Corridor separated Germany from East Prussia.

Task

12 Explain why the Nazi–Soviet Pact would help Hitler in his invasion of Poland.

Hint

For Task 12, use a map as well as the text.

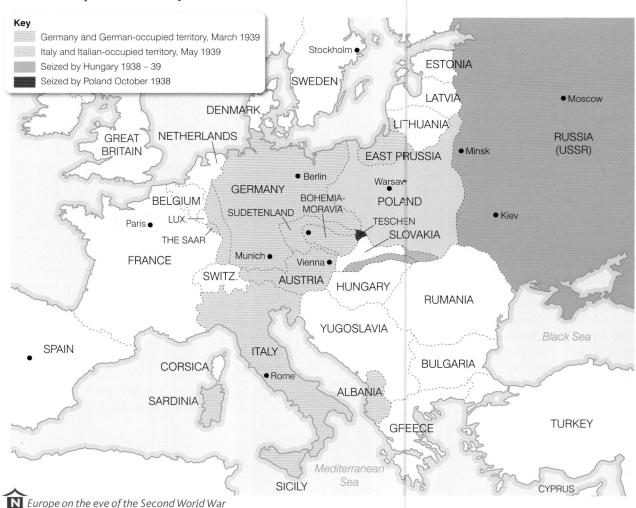

Key
- Germany and German-occupied territory, March 1939
- Italy and Italian-occupied territory, May 1939
- Seized by Hungary 1938 – 39
- Seized by Poland October 1938

N *Europe on the eve of the Second World War*

- If Britain kept the guarantee to defend Poland, war was inevitable.
- Britain and France had lost another possible ally in the USSR. Hitler had convinced Stalin that there would be no war and he would regain lost Soviet lands. Many historians believe that Stalin had been fooled by Hitler; some historians argue that he still expected Hitler to attack the Soviet Union and the pact gave him time to prepare his armies to defend against this attack when it came in 1941.

O 'Rendezvous': a British cartoon on the Nazi–Soviet Pact, 20 September 1939

Task

13 Study Source **O**.

a   Explain the meaning of the cartoon. What does it suggest about the Nazi–Soviet Pact?

b   What is represented by the figure on the ground between Hitler and Stalin?

c   How accurate is the cartoon? Explain your answer by referring to the purpose of the source as well as using its content and your knowledge.

Poland and the outbreak of war

Hitler had long wanted Danzig as its population was over 90 per cent German. As early as April 1939 he demanded that the Poles handed it over. Hitler believed that if he kept the pressure on Poland, Britain and France would come to a similar agreement with him as they had at Munich over the Sudetenland. He still believed that Britain and France were so afraid of war that they would back down, especially as his claim to Danzig was far more justified than any claim he had to Czechoslovakia, and they had not opposed him over that. Poland, strengthened by the guarantee of independence given to them by Britain and France after the collapse of Czechoslovakia earlier in 1939, refused to give in to Hitler's demands.

Much to Hitler's surprise, Britain warned him that it would join the war if Germany invaded Poland. There was no hope of another Munich. Hitler had gone too far. The collapse of Czechoslovakia in March 1939 proved to be the last straw for the appeasers. Public opinion in Britain was in favour of opposing Hitler. On 1 September 1939 German troops invaded Poland. On 3 September Britain declared war on Germany. Britain was unable to defend Poland, which was overrun by Germany and the USSR within four weeks. Hitler was convinced even then that Britain would accept his gains in Poland and not continue the war. He was mistaken.

∞links

Look back at pages 59–63 for the Munich Agreement and the collapse of Czechoslovakia.

Activity

This activity could be completed as a discussion, debate or group activity.

1 a What was the contribution of each of the following to the outbreak of the Second World War?
   i   The Treaty of Versailles
   ii Hitler's aims and policies
   iii Britain's failure to support the League of Nations
   iv Chamberlain's policy of appeasement
   v   The policy of the USSR
  b Which do you think was the main reason? Explain your answer.

Did you know ??????

The points given in the activity cover two chapters. The bullet-point question on this topic will involve two points from this chapter alone. They must be points that are named in the specification, which are the main headings in this chapter. You must make sure that you can assess the effect of all these.

Practice questions

Study **Source A** and then answer all three questions that follow.

Source A   British cartoon published after the Munich conference. The figure on the left is Neville Chamberlain, the British Prime Minister. On the right, 'John Bull' represents Britain

A GREAT MEDIATOR

John Bull. "I've known many Prime Ministers in my time, Sir, but never one who worked so hard for security in the face of such terrible odds."

1   In August 1939 Hitler made an agreement with Stalin – the Nazi–Soviet Pact. Explain how the Nazi–Soviet Pact of August 1939 led to the outbreak of war in September 1939. *(4 marks)*

2   **Source A** suggests that the Munich Agreement had been a success.

Do you agree with this view?

Explain your answer by referring to the purpose of the source as well as using its content and your knowledge. *(6 marks)*

3   Which was the bigger threat to European peace in the 1930s:

- the remilitarisation of the Rhineland in 1936;
- the Anschluss with Austria in 1938?

You must refer to **both** events when explaining your answer. *(10 marks)*

4.1 Why did the USA and USSR become rivals in the years 1945–49?

A *An atomic explosion*

Objectives

In this chapter you will learn about:

the end of the Second World War

the reasons for the division of Europe into east and west

the impact of the atom bomb and the start of the nuclear arms race

the Korean War

the reasons for a 'thaw' in relations.

The Second World War ended in 1945 with the surrender of Germany in May and the dropping of the atom bomb in August forcing Japan to surrender. At the end of 1944 Hitler had launched one last offensive in the west but Germany could not compete against the extra resources of the Allies and the Allied advance continued. In the east, Soviet troops entered Berlin, which the Germans defended to the last, but in the end Hitler committed suicide and the Germans were forced to surrender. Europe had been left devastated by the war.

Timeline

From Yalta to the Warsaw Pact

Feb	1945	Yalta Conference
May	1945	Germany defeated
Jul	1945	Potsdam Conference
Aug	1945	Atom bomb dropped on Hiroshima
Mar	1946	Iron Curtain Speech
Mar	1947	Truman Doctrine
Jun	1947	Marshall Plan announced
Sep	1947	Cominform set up by Stalin
Feb	1948	Communist takeover of Czechoslovakia
Jun	1948	Yugoslavia expelled from Cominform; Berlin Blockade begins
Apr	1949	Formation of NATO
May	1949	Berlin Blockade lifted
Jun	1950	Outbreak of Korean War
Nov	1952	Testing of first hydrogen bomb
Mar	1953	Death of Stalin
Jul	1953	Ceasefire in Korea
	1953–56	The 'Thaw'
May	1955	Warsaw Pact

Since 1941, when Germany invaded Soviet Russia, Britain had joined with the USSR and USA to win the war. As the war was coming to an end, the two new superpowers, the USSR and USA, began to show their differences. This led to the Cold War. This was a war of threats and propaganda rather than direct fighting between the USSR and USA. The tension during the period was increased by the development of nuclear weapons and the fears that this caused.

Ideological differences

The USA did not return to its policy of isolation in 1945; it played its full part in the reorganisation of Europe. Before the war, there were several Great Powers. The war clearly left the USA and USSR as the strongest powers in the world – the new superpowers. They had fought on the same side in the Second World War, united by Hitler's policies, but the alliance was an uneasy one. Even towards the end of the war, suspicions between them began to grow. This was because they had different political systems and different **ideologies**. These ideological differences are summarised in Table **B**.

> **Key terms**
>
> **Ideology:** a set of beliefs and characteristics.

B *The ideological differences between the USA and USSR*

Aspect	USA	USSR
Type of government	Democratic – elected by the people who had a choice of candidates from different parties.	One party dictatorship – people could only vote for communists.
Economic system	Capitalist – private individuals owned industry and kept the profits.	Communist – everything owned by the state.
Individual rights	The freedom and rights of each person were considered important and Americans objected to the state interfering in their lives.	Individual rights were closely controlled by the state because the most important thing was the good of society as a whole.

Activities

Answering these questions should help you to understand why Communism was suspicious of democracy and why the West could not trust the USSR.

1 Russia had not only been invaded in 1941 by Germany but also in the First World War and by France in 1812. Try to find out the number of Russians who died as a result of these wars.

2 Look for other examples of actions by the West in the 20th century that would have aroused suspicions that they wanted to get rid of Communism in the USSR.

3 Had the communist governments in Soviet Russia done anything to arouse the suspicions of the West?

Hint

Research Russia's withdrawal from the First World War and foreign intervention in the Russian Civil War of 1918–21.

∞ links

See page 59 for the Munich Conference and page 64 for the Nazi–Soviet Pact.

These differences led to different policies, which aroused fears in the minds of Americans and Soviets. Both felt that their way of life was the correct one and had suspicions that they each wanted to impose their own system of government on the world. For example, at the end of the war, Stalin, the Soviet leader, tried to get as much territory for the USSR and Communism as he could. The Americans and the West thought that this was because Stalin wanted 'World Communism' – that is, the spread of Communism throughout the world. Churchill issued several warnings about the danger of allowing the Soviets to take control of countries in Europe by setting up communist governments in them. Now that Communism had been achieved in the USSR, the West felt that Stalin was trying to strengthen the Soviet position in Europe by occupying as much of Germany as was possible and by taking land from other countries that had been occupied by the Germans during the war.

On the other hand, the Soviets claimed that all Stalin wanted to do was to protect the USSR from future invasion. Some of the actions of the Allies during the war had aroused Stalin's suspicions. The Americans had delayed in opening a second front in Europe by invading France to relieve pressure on the USSR. Stalin thought that this was because they wanted Soviet Russia to be exhausted by fighting the Germans, leaving the USSR open to attack. Stalin tried to prevent further attacks on the USSR by building a 'buffer zone' of states friendly to the USSR between the USSR and the democratic countries in the West.

■ The Yalta Conference

This conference was held just before the end of the war to decide what to do with Germany after its defeat. Yalta is in the Crimea, part of the USSR, and the conference was attended by Stalin, Roosevelt (the American President) and Churchill (the British Prime Minister). The meeting was regarded as a success and the leaders agreed on the following:

- Germany was to be divided into four zones occupied by Britain, France, the USA and USSR.
- Although Berlin, the capital of Germany, was in the Soviet zone, it was also to be divided into four zones of occupation.
- Nazi war criminals were to be hunted down and tried for their crimes.

- Free elections were to be held in the states of Eastern Europe once they had been freed from German control.

- Stalin agreed to enter the war against Japan in return for Soviet gains in the Far East.

- A United Nations (UN) organisation should be set up to replace the League of Nations and to keep peace. This was established at a later conference in San Francisco in April 1945.

- Germany should pay reparations for the war, but the amount was to be decided later.

There was some disagreement over the government and frontiers of Poland once it had been freed from Nazi occupation. This was to cause problems later.

> **Did you know** ??????
>
> Each leader had an agenda for the Yalta Conference: Roosevelt wanted Soviet support in the American Pacific War against Japan; Churchill wanted free elections and democratic governments in Eastern Europe; Stalin wanted Soviet influence in Eastern Europe.

C *The 'Big Three' at Yalta: Churchill, Roosevelt and Stalin*

The Potsdam Conference

This conference was held after the defeat of Germany, but while the war against Japan was still going on. There had been several changes between Yalta and Potsdam which altered the relationship between the three powers.

Roosevelt had died in April 1945 and was replaced by Truman, who was more suspicious of Stalin and did not get on as well with him. Roosevelt had been prepared to negotiate with Stalin, but Truman hated Communism and wanted to be tough with him. Churchill was defeated in a general election in Britain and replaced by Attlee. The biggest change was what had happened in Poland. Soviet troops had occupied most of Eastern Europe and stayed there. Part of East Germany was taken over by the new communist government in Poland, which had the support of Stalin. There had been no free elections. This was against what had been agreed at Yalta. On 16 July the Americans successfully tested the atom bomb. Stalin was not told immediately and it was clear that the USA was not going to share the secret with its allies. This increased Stalin's suspicions.

The division of Germany and the treatment of war criminals agreed at Yalta were confirmed at Potsdam. However, the cooperation of wartime had come to an end. The alliance between the USSR and the West appeared over. On reparations it was decided that each country could take its own reparations from its own occupied zone, but the Western powers did allow the USSR to receive industrial equipment and goods from their zones.

D *The 'Big Three' at Potsdam: Attlee, Truman and Stalin*

Tasks

1. What were the main differences between the Yalta and Potsdam Conferences? Explain your answer.

2. Look at the list of what was agreed at Yalta on pages 70 and 71.

   a. Which of these had been ignored by Stalin in the months between Yalta and Potsdam? Explain his reasons for this.

   b. What effect did this have on the relationship between the USA and USSR?

■ The dropping of the atom bomb and its effects

The Americans were suffering massive casualties in taking the Japanese islands and defeating Japan. To prevent further casualties, President Truman made the decision to use the atom bomb. On 10 August 1945 the war against Japan ended after the USA dropped atom bombs on Hiroshima (6 August) and Nagasaki (9 August). Stalin had promised to declare war on Japan in return for receiving territory in the Far East at the Yalta Conference in February, but he had delayed entering the war against Japan. Truman informed Churchill at Yalta about the USA's proposed use of the atom bomb on Japan, but although Stalin was made aware of the successful testing of the bomb, he was not told that the Americans planned to use it against Japan. The Soviets did join the war against Japan on 8 August and made some gains in the Far East, but they were not allowed to share in the defeat of Japan.

Did you know ??????

The code name of the atom bomb dropped on Hiroshima was 'Little Boy'; the code name of the bomb dropped on Nagasaki was 'Fat Man'.

Did you know ??????

The atom bombs killed as many as 140,000 people in Hiroshima and 80,000 in Nagasaki by the end of 1945. Roughly half were killed on the days of the bombings. Thousands more have since died from injuries or illnesses caused by exposure to radiation from the bombs.

E *Models of Hiroshima before and after the atom bomb*

Tasks

3 Use Source **E** to describe what happened to Hiroshima as a result of the dropping of the atom bomb.

4 What do you think happened to the people living in Hiroshima and Nagasaki when the bombs were dropped?

5 Why could Stalin not risk a war against the USA after 6 August 1945?

6 What do you think Stalin instructed his scientists to develop after the defeat of Japan?

The Iron Curtain: Soviet expansion in the East

The USSR and Communism expanded after the Second World War. Stalin was determined to build his 'buffer' states on the western frontier, which would prevent any future invasion of Soviet Russia. As each state was freed from the Nazis by the Soviet armies, the army remained in control and communist governments that supported the USSR were set up. At Yalta, the powers had agreed that all the countries freed from German control should be allowed to decide their own government in free elections. What happened in the countries freed by the USSR did not follow this principle, as shown in Table **F**.

∞links

The Yalta Conference is covered on pages 70 and 71.

F *Soviet expansion in Eastern Europe, 1944–49*

Country	Type of government	Action taken
Albania	Communists took control in 1944.	Little opposition.
Bulgaria	Communist coalition took power in 1944.	The communists executed leaders of other parties.
Czechoslovakia	Coalition government freely elected in 1946. Communists seized power in 1948 before elections.	The USSR purged the civil service. Masaryk was murdered and the security police moved in.
East Germany	Ruled directly by the USSR until 1949 when it became the communist German Democratic Republic.	Industrial machinery and resources were moved to the USSR. Scientists and technicians moved to the USSR.
Hungary	In 1945 communists got only 17% of the vote. In 1948 Communist rule was established.	Opposition was stamped out.
Poland	Coalition set up but dominated by communists who were unpopular and ruled alone from 1947.	The USSR refused to have free elections.
Romania	Communist People's Republic formed in 1947.	The king was forced to abdicate.
Yugoslavia	Tito elected president in 1945 – a communist who was not controlled by the USSR.	Expelled from Cominform by the USSR in 1948.

Churchill appeared to fear this Soviet advance as early as 1945. He wanted the Allies to make a dash for Berlin and take it before the Russians could get there. Later in a letter to Truman in May 1945, he warned him of the danger of the Soviet Union, claiming that 'an iron curtain is being drawn upon their front'. Truman did not seem concerned at first, even when Churchill repeated the expression in his famous Iron Curtain Speech which he made in the USA in 1946. In this speech Churchill called for an alliance of the West to resist the expansion of the USSR in the East. The name Iron Curtain has been used since to mean the imaginary line drawn between Communism in the East and the democratic governments of the West.

∞links

For more information on Masaryk, see page 77.

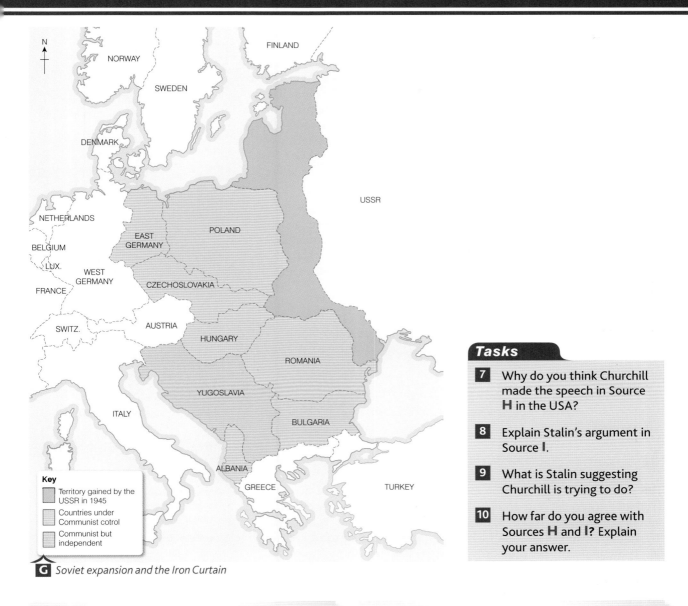

G Soviet expansion and the Iron Curtain

Key
- Territory gained by the USSR in 1945
- Countries under Communist cotrol
- Communist but independent

Tasks

7 Why do you think Churchill made the speech in Source **H** in the USA?

8 Explain Stalin's argument in Source **I**.

9 What is Stalin suggesting Churchill is trying to do?

10 How far do you agree with Sources **H** and **I**? Explain your answer.

> 66 *A shadow has fallen upon the scenes so lately lighted by the Allied victory. Nobody knows what Soviet Russia intends to do in the immediate future or what are the limits to their expansive tendencies. From Stettin on the Baltic to Trieste on the Adriatic, an iron curtain has descended across the Continent. Behind that line lie all the capitals of Central and Eastern Europe … and all are subject to a very high measure of control from Moscow.* 99

H Churchill's Iron Curtain Speech, which he made to an American audience that included President Truman

> 66 *Mr Churchill now stands as a firebrand of war. As a result of the German invasion the Soviet Union has lost about seven million people. In other words, several times more than Britain and the United States together. The Germans made their invasion of the USSR through Finland, Poland and Romania. What can there be surprising about the fact that the Soviet Union, anxious for its future safety, is trying to see to it that governments loyal to the Soviet Union should exist in these countries?* 99

I Stalin's reply to Churchill's speech

■ The Truman Doctrine

Truman eventually showed his open opposition to Communism after events in Greece where there was civil war. In 1944 British troops freed Greece from Nazi control and restored the monarchy. Since then Britain had been helping the Greek King in the fight against communists who were trying to take over the country. Elections had taken place in 1946 and the parties that supported the monarchy were successful. This was not accepted by the communists, who continued their resistance using guerrilla tactics against the government. The communists were being helped by Albania, Bulgaria and Yugoslavia.

By 1947 Britain was unable to continue its support for the monarchy and informed the Americans of this. The Greek Civil War made Truman realise that the only way of checking this aggressive behaviour by communists in Europe was by using American resources. It is this realisation that was the immediate cause of the statement made by Truman on 12 March 1947, which became known as the Truman Doctrine.

> **"** *I believe that it must be the policy of the United States to support free peoples who are resisting attempted* **subjugation** *by armed minorities or by outside pressures.*
>
> *The free peoples of the world look to us for support in maintaining those freedoms. If we falter in our leadership, we may endanger the peace of the world.* **"**

J *The Truman Doctrine, 12 March 1947*

This was Truman's justification for helping Greece. Congress accepted Truman's argument and granted $400 million, which was used to support Greece and Turkey against communist influence. Turkey was a neighbour of Greece and the USSR. It controlled the **Dardanelles** and had come under threat from Soviet Russia, who had moved troops to its border with Turkey. If Turkey came under the influence of the USSR, then Greece would have been isolated and surrounded by Communism. Britain and the USA had supported Turkey during the war. Turkey now asked for further funds for modernisation. Britain was still recovering from the war and Truman argued that only the USA could afford to give it this money, which would save Turkey from becoming communist.

With the help of American arms and money, the communist threat in Greece was defeated by 1949 and Turkey was able to resist pressure from the USSR, particularly over the Dardanelles. The Truman Doctrine began a new era in American foreign policy. It showed that the USA was not going to revert to isolation and Truman made it clear that the USA would aim to stop the spread of Communism throughout the world. This became known as the 'policy of containment'. Communism would be contained within its existing boundaries and not allowed to spread. Although the USSR was not mentioned in Truman's appeal to Congress for aid for Greece and Turkey, it was clear that opposition to the spreading influence of the Soviet Union was his main concern. On account of this, many communists felt that it was a declaration of war against Communism and so regarded it as the start of the Cold War.

Key terms

Subjugation: conquest.

Dardanelles: part of the strategic waterway linking the Mediterranean to the Black Sea.

Task

11 Explain why the USSR was concerned about the Truman Doctrine (Source **J**).

The Marshall Plan

The Marshall Plan was the other half of the Truman Doctrine. The economies of Europe had been ruined by the Second World War and governments in France and Italy were being threatened by strong communist parties. Truman sent George Marshall to Europe to see the situation first-hand. He reported back that Europe would need around $17 billion to aid its recovery. Congress was on the point of refusing this when events in Czechoslovakia played a part. In 1948 the communists carried out a purge of non-communists and Jan Masaryk, a minister who supported the West, was murdered. The communists took full control in Czechoslovakia. This decided Congress: they granted the money.

Marshall Aid certainly rescued the economies of the West. It was given to 16 countries and was used first of all to improve agriculture and then to build up industry. Britain and France received the most. Stalin prevented any communist countries in the East from receiving it. President Tito in Yugoslavia defied Stalin and received Marshall Aid, and as a result was expelled from Cominform in 1948. The Soviets claimed that the Marshall Plan was dollar imperialism: the Americans were using dollars to bribe European countries so that they would become dependent on the USA and join them against the USSR. In this way it increased suspicions between the USSR and USA and contributed to the Cold War.

The generosity of the USA did much to bring about the recovery of Western Europe. The Americans certainly wanted to help, but they also realised that the recovery of Europe was in their own interests. They needed European markets to recover to avoid another depression such as the one that had occurred in the 1930s. It was also seen as a means

> **Did you know** ??????
>
> The Marshall Plan did not always have a positive effect. For example, France was required to show American films in return for receiving financial assistance from the USA, which damaged the French film industry.

> 66 *The seeds of Communism spread and grow in the evil soil of poverty.*
>
> *The Marshall Plan is directed not against any country or doctrine but against hunger, poverty, desperation and chaos. Its purpose should be the revival of a working economy in the world so as to permit the emergence of political and social conditions in which free institutions can exist.* 99

K *Extracts from George Marshall's speech, June 1947*

M *This poster won first prize in a competition sponsored by the European Recovery Programme. The aim of the poster was to capture the goals and spirit of the Marshall Plan*

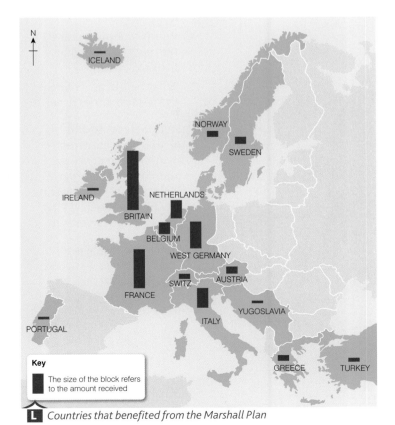

Key

The size of the block refers to the amount received

L *Countries that benefited from the Marshall Plan*

of holding back Communism, which the Americans believed thrived where there was poverty.

N A demonstration in Germany against the Marshall Plan

O 'The Wind from the West', a British cartoon of 14 July 1948

Tasks

12 Do you agree with Marshall in Source **K** about the reasons for the Marshall Plan? Explain your answer.

13 Study Source **L**.
 a Which countries received the most aid from the Marshall Plan?
 b What type of government do these countries have?

14 Study Sources **M** and **N**, which are both from countries that benefited from the Marshall Plan. Explain why one appears to support the Marshall Plan and the other opposes it.

15 Explain the meaning of Source **O**. Does it support or oppose the Marshall Plan? Explain your answer.

Cominform and Comecon

Stalin's reaction to the Truman Doctrine and Marshall Plan was to set up Cominform (the Communist Information Bureau) in September 1947. All the communist parties in Europe were involved in this and it was intended to defend Communism against the aggression of the USA. It increased Stalin's control of communist states in Eastern Europe. They were to be **satellite states** of the USSR. Plans for recovery were established and members were expected to trade with each other, not the West. When Yugoslavia showed too much independence, Stalin expelled it from Cominform and Yugoslavia followed its own brand of Communism under President Tito. The USSR offered aid to the satellite states in 1949 with the introduction of Comecon. This was intended to unite the economies of the communist states but, in fact, it increased the control that Stalin had over them.

The Berlin Blockade

The first main crisis of the Cold War occurred in Germany. At Yalta, it had been agreed that Germany should pay reparations to the Allies for damage caused during the war. When the war had ended, the USSR confiscated many of the resources of its zone. Stalin wanted to keep Germany weak.

The Soviet advance in Eastern Europe changed the view of the Americans. Truman began to think that a recovered Germany would be a good barrier to the expansion of the USSR. Accordingly, Germany was given Marshall Aid to enable economic recovery to take place. In 1948 the three western zones were merged to form one and preparations were made for an independent state of West Germany to be set up. This alarmed the Soviets. The difference between the relative prosperity of the western zones thanks to Marshall Aid and the poverty of the east was clear.

In 1948 Britain and America decided to set up a new currency for West Germany. The USSR was not involved in this decision and Stalin argued that it was against what had been agreed at Potsdam. This was the excuse he needed to show his power. Berlin had been divided into four zones – like the rest of Germany – but it was 160 km inside the Soviet zone. The Western powers were given free access to West Berlin through the Soviet zone. West Berlin was recovering; East Berlin was still weak. Stalin decided that the whole of Berlin should belong to the Soviets.

By 23 June 1948 all routes into West Berlin had been closed by Stalin. This meant that no food supplies could reach West Berlin. His plan was to force the West to withdraw from Berlin by starving the people of West Berlin.

links

For Yugoslavia and the Marshall Plan, see page 77.

Key terms

Satellite state: a country that is independent, but under the heavy influence or control of another country.

Did you know ??????

Stalin closed the routes in and out of West Berlin under the pretext of 'technical difficulties'. America and Britain had never negotiated an agreement to safeguard their access to West Berlin, leaving them powerless.

The Berlin Airlift

The Berlin Blockade posed a problem for the Americans. Truman was not prepared to allow his policy of containment to fail. The Americans feared that if they gave way on West Berlin, the Soviets would threaten West Germany next. West Berlin had about six weeks of fuel and food left. The people would starve unless the USA handed over West Berlin to the Soviets or provided them with food and other essentials such as fuel. How could the Americans help them? If they had forced their way into the city using tanks, it would have looked as if they had been the aggressors and could cause a war. They decided to use the three air routes into West Berlin and take goods in by air. It was estimated that at least 4,000 tonnes of supplies would be needed every day.

At first, the British and American planes were only flying in 600 tonnes a day. However, once the pilots had got used to the narrow air corridors, the number of deliveries increased and 8,000 tonnes a day were being flown in day and night by 1949. The pilots had to put up with ice and fog as well as being tracked by Soviet fighter planes that were ensuring that they did not stray out of the air zones. Seventy-nine American and British pilots and German ground crew lost their lives during the airlift.

Stalin tried all he knew to persuade the West Berliners to give up the struggle. In the winter of 1948, the electricity supplies were cut off. Stalin promised the West Berliners extra rations if they moved to the East, but only about 2 per cent of the population accepted his bribe. Stalin considered attacking the American and British planes, but realised that if he did it would be a declaration of war and he was afraid of the American nuclear weapons. On 12 May 1949 Stalin accepted that his plan had failed and lifted the blockade.

⬭ links

For more on the policy of containment see page 76.

Key
Key to occupied zones
- ☐ UK
- ▨ USSR
- ▨ USA
- ▨ France

Q *Air corridors used by British and American planes*

P *Berliners watching as an Allied plane brings in supplies*

Did you know ? ? ? ? ? ?

Gail Halvorsen, an American pilot, began dropping chocolate to Berlin children during the airlift. This developed into a larger operation with the support of American confectionery companies. The planes dropping treats were called 'Raisin Bombers' by German children.

The importance of the Berlin Blockade and Airlift

- The USA and the West had proved that they were prepared to stand up to the USSR and resist any further expansion – the Truman Doctrine in action.

- It ended any possibility of a speedy unification, not only of Berlin but also of Germany. In 1949 it was divided into the pro-West republic of West Germany and the pro-Soviet communist East Germany.

- It was seen as a victory in the West and led to the formation of NATO.

- It was the first main crisis of the Cold War and set the pattern for the future – it consisted of threats, not war, but deepened the hostility between West and East.

R   *A British cartoon, July 1948, showing Stalin as 'The Bird Watcher'*

Tasks

16   Why do you think Stalin blockaded West Berlin in 1948–49?

17   Why do you think the Allies airlifted goods to Berlin?

18   How do Sources **P**, **Q** and **R** help you to learn about the Berlin Airlift?

19   What is Source **R** suggesting about Stalin and the airlift?

20   Explain how Source **R** shows that it is biased.

Activity

This activity could be completed as a discussion, debate or group activity.

4 a   Which of the following contributed most to the start of the Cold War?

- i   Ideological differences between the USSR and USA
- ii   The Yalta and Potsdam Conferences
- iii   The atom bomb
- iv   Soviet expansion in Eastern Europe
- v   The Truman Doctrine and Marshall Plan
- vi   The Berlin Blockade and Airlift

b   Which do you think was the main reason? Explain your answer.

Study tip

This activity contains an obvious stem for the bullet-point question. All the points mentioned in the activity are named in the specification, so any two of them could be included in a question. You could also have one of them with an event from 1949–55.

The formation of NATO

The Berlin Blockade convinced the Americans that the West needed a common defence strategy to oppose any acts of aggression. This led to the signing of the North Atlantic Treaty Organization (NATO) in April 1949. This was a military pact in which all the countries agreed to help each other against any act of aggression. It was to have an army with a common command. In 1949 it had 12 members: the USA, Britain, France, Italy, Belgium, Holland, Luxembourg, Denmark, Norway, Iceland, Portugal and Canada. This was later extended by the entry of Greece and Turkey in 1952 and West Germany in 1955. It meant that the Americans could build air bases in Western Europe where planes equipped with nuclear bombs could be stationed ready for use in the event of an act of aggression from another power.

> **Did you know** ??????
> The first NATO Secretary General, Lord Ismay, famously stated that the organisation's goal was 'to keep the Russians out, the Americans in, and the Germans down'.

> **Did you know** ??????
> In 1954, the USSR suggested that it should join NATO to preserve peace in Europe. The NATO member countries, fearing that the Soviet Union's motive was to weaken the alliance, rejected this proposal.

A Ernest Bevin, the British Foreign Minister, signs the NATO agreement for Britain, April 1949

> 66 Like others, my country has had forced upon it the task of fighting two world wars against aggression within a quarter of a century. Today will bring a feeling of relief. At last democracy is no longer a series of isolated units. 99
>
> **B** Ernest Bevin speaking on the formation of NATO

> 66 The North Atlantic Treaty is not about the self-defence of states. These states are not threatened by anyone and no one intends to attack them. On the contrary, the Treaty has an aggressive characteristic and is aimed against the USSR. 99
>
> **C** Soviet protest note on the formation of NATO

Task

1 Study Sources **B** and **C**.

a How do they differ in their view of NATO?

b Why do you think they differ in this way?

c Which of them is more accurate? Give reasons for your answer.

■ The nuclear arms race

The dropping of the atom bombs on Hiroshima and Nagasaki in 1945 started the nuclear arms race between the two superpowers. This became a major theme of the Cold War. People began to believe that the more nuclear weapons you had, the more powerful you were as a country. The nuclear arms race was how the USA and the USSR made sure that they did not get left behind in the number of nuclear weapons they possessed, so they would never be disadvantaged. This competition for arms became very expensive for both countries as they tried to increase their stockpiles of nuclear weapons and develop deadlier and more effective weapons.

Until 1949 the USA had the advantage: the USSR would not risk a war against the USA because of the destructive power of the bomb. In 1949 the USSR exploded its first atomic bomb. The hydrogen bomb, a more powerful bomb that could destroy the whole of Moscow, was successfully tested by the Americans in 1952. This H-bomb was much smaller than the bombs used in 1945 but more than 2,000 times more powerful. The Soviets responded with their own hydrogen bomb in 1953. Both countries felt that they had to continue this race to protect themselves. They both tried to keep ahead in the race.

Did you know ??????

John Foster Dulles, the American Secretary of State, called the Nuclear Arms Race 'brinkmanship', meaning that each side was pushing a dangerous situation to the verge of disaster in order to achieve its goals.

Task

2 How do you think testing the hydrogen bomb would affect the Cold War?

D *Testing the hydrogen bomb*

The Korean War

At the end of the Second World War, Korea was freed from Japanese control. North Korea was occupied by Soviet soldiers; South Korea by American soldiers. It was agreed that there should be free elections and Korea should be united in the future. The Americans supported this because two-thirds of the population of Korea lived in the south and so they felt that the communist north would be outvoted. By 1948 this proved impossible and two independent states of North and South Korea were set up, divided by the 38th Parallel. Elections were held in the south, which resulted in South Korea being ruled by an anti-communist government led by Syngman Rhee with its capital at Seoul. The Soviets set up the communist government of North Korea under Kim Il Sung, with its capital at Pyongyang. Although Soviet and American troops left in 1949, North Korea was still supported by the USSR and South Korea by the USA.

The victory of the communists in China under Mao Zedong in 1949 meant that North Korea had a border with another communist state. The Koreans were not satisfied with the division of their country and both Syngman Rhee and Kim Il Sung claimed to be the ruler of the whole country. This was likely to cause problems in the future. What caused the war that followed to break out is uncertain. Stalin certainly encouraged the North Koreans and supplied them with tanks and planes and the communists in China probably urged the North Koreans to attack. The communists claimed that they were acting to protect themselves because troops from South Korea had crossed the 38th Parallel.

The North Korean advance

The North Koreans attacked South Korea in 1950 and advanced quickly, crossing the 38th Parallel and capturing the capital Seoul. They soon occupied the whole of South Korea except the south-east corner known as the Pusan pocket. This was a problem for Truman and the Americans. The USSR had tested the atom bomb in 1949 and Communism had been successful in China, so the Americans thought they were losing the Cold War. Following so quickly after the Berlin Blockade, Truman and the Americans considered that events in Korea were part of a grand plan by the USSR to spread Communism throughout the world. They believed in the **Domino Effect** and felt that they had to resist the spread of Communism. This was to be the Truman Doctrine and its policy of containment in action.

The Americans referred the invasion to the Security Council of the UN, but began to move their troops in Japan to Korea before a decision was made by the UN. The Security Council appealed to North Korea to withdraw its troops from the south and, when this was ignored, declared that North Korea was the aggressor and called on all member states to send help to the South. The USSR would have used its veto if it had been present, but it was refusing to attend the UN because the new communist China had not been accepted as a member.

Task

3 Look at a map of the world and find Korea.

a Explain the importance of Korea's position in the world.

b Why was the USA interested in Korea's future in 1950?

Key terms

Domino Effect: the belief that if one country became communist, those next to it would fall to Communism like a pack of dominoes.

UN intervention

A UN army made up of contributions from 16 nations was sent to Korea. It was led by the American General Douglas MacArthur. Most of the troops were American, and Truman saw it as part of the Truman Doctrine to contain Communism. The North Koreans were surprised by American marines, who landed at Inchon and cut off their supplies. The North Koreans were forced to retreat. At this stage, Truman went beyond containment. With UN backing, American troops invaded North Korea, captured Pyongyang and occupied two-thirds of the country. They soon reached the Yalu River – the border with communist China.

Key profile	
General Douglas MacArthur	
1880	Born 26 January in Arkansas
1917	Fights in the First World War; decorated 13 times for bravery
1942	Receives the Medal of Honor for services in the Philippines
1945	Accepts the surrender of Japan and organises its occupation
1950	Leads the UN forces in Korea
1951	Removed from office by Truman
1964	Dies 5 April

E US marines advancing in Korea

F North Korean advance

G The UN and South Korean offensive

Final advances of the Korean War

China was now concerned about the American advance and decided to help the North Koreans. About 250,000 Chinese troops, described as volunteers, entered Korea. There were too many of them for the Americans and, by January 1951, they had driven the UN troops out of North Korea and once again captured Seoul. MacArthur wanted to launch an all-out attack on China using the atom bomb. Truman felt that this would cause a major war, so he dismissed MacArthur and decided to go back to his policy of containing Communism. By June 1951 UN troops had driven the communists out of South Korea and defended the frontier. Peace talks began in 1951 and there was very little fighting for the next two years. It was agreed in 1953 that the frontier would remain along the 38th Parallel.

The war proved to be costly for Korea: the country had been devastated by the fighting, about 4 million soldiers and civilians had been killed and 5 million became homeless. American losses were around 50,000, with other UN troops losing about 17,000. The Chinese suffered about 900,000 casualties.

> 66 *The attack upon the Republic of Korea makes it plain beyond doubt that the international Communist movement is prepared to use armed invasion to conquer independent nations.* 99

H *President Truman warns the nation, 1950*

> 66 *The American military intervention in Korea in the summer of 1950 aggravated the already tense international relations. The United States, having landed troops in Southern Korea after Japan's surrender in 1945, was seeking to gain control of the whole country.* 99

I *A Soviet view of the Korean War*

Did you know ??????

Towards the end of the Korean War, public opinion ratings of Truman were at the lowest ever recorded for any US president until George W. Bush.

Tasks

4 Why do you think General MacArthur was popular in the USA in 1950?

5 What does Source **E** tell you about the fighting in Korea?

6 What was the purpose of President Truman's speech in Source **H**?

7 Source **I** gives a reason for the intervention of the USA in Korea. Do you agree that this was the main reason? Explain your answer.

Hint

For Task 7, use your knowledge to explain how far you agree and disagree with Source **I**. Examine the provenance of the source: does the writer have any reason to want to stress this point of view?

The importance of the Korean War

- It extended the Cold War to the Far East. China also helped communist rebels in Indo-China (Vietnam) against the French.
- It indicated that Truman was prepared to stick to the Truman Doctrine and to the principle of containing Communism.
- At the same time, it appeared that the superpowers did not want to make the Cold War into a 'hot' war: the Soviets did not become directly involved. Some Americans agreed with MacArthur and wanted to take the war to Communism, but Truman refused to support MacArthur and the war did not spread beyond Korea.
- It marked the emergence of communist China as a world power. The Chinese had prevented the USA from uniting Korea and China became more friendly with the USSR.
- The UN had resisted an act of aggression – something that the League of Nations had never been able to do – but it was condemned as a capitalist tool by the communists because its forces had fought against Communism under the leadership of the USA.
- The USSR had not been directly involved in the war, although it did supply weapons to the North Koreans.
- Korea was still divided as North and South and it appeared as if the division was now permanent.

Study tip

You need to know the details of the Korean War because it could be part of a 'describe' question. However, how it affected the Cold War is more important and it could be a bullet point in the extended writing question.

The 'Thaw'

The death of Stalin in 1953 led to a new direction in Soviet foreign policy. Now that East and West had the power of the hydrogen bomb, it seemed sensible to ease the tension of the Cold War. The Americans were willing to negotiate because they regarded Stalin as the main cause of the Cold War. This new cooperation was first seen in the support that the USSR gave to ending the Korean War. This was followed in 1955 when the Soviets agreed to sign the Austrian State Treaty, which ended the occupation of Austria that had continued since 1945. Austria had been divided into four zones at the end of the Second World War and the Soviets had taken many food supplies in reparations from their zone. This now came to an end: Austria became independent and was restored to its 1937 frontiers.

The new Soviet leadership was at first a coalition but eventually Khrushchev emerged as the leader. He appeared to be keen to make a fresh start with the West. He argued that in the days of the hydrogen bomb, the ideas of supporting a communist revolution in other parts of the world were over. It was necessary to live in peace with the West, even if the Soviets did not like its ideals and policies. In 1956 he used the phrase 'peaceful co-existence' to describe these policies. He showed his willingness to be friendly to the West by his visits to Britain and the USA. A Summit Conference was held in Geneva in 1955 – the first since 1945. This was attended by the leaders of America, China, Britain, France and the USSR. Very little was agreed but it was seen as a turning point in the Cold War. East and West were meeting and talking together.

Did you know ??????

Issues discussed at the Geneva Summit Conference included trade agreements, international security and disarmament, and German unification.

Tasks

8 Explain what Khrushchev meant in Source **J**.

9 Study Source **K**.

a What can we learn about the importance of Stalin in the USSR from this source?

b Why would this make change difficult in the USSR after his death?

66 *There are only two ways: either peaceful co-existence or the most destructive war in history. There is no third way.* 99

J *Khrushchev's secret speech, 1956*

K *Stalin's body lying in state in the USSR*

The Warsaw Pact

In 1955 West Germany joined NATO. This revived Soviet concern about the re-emergence of Germany and led to the formation of the Warsaw Pact. This pact was a military alliance for mutual defence, which the USSR signed along with Poland, Czechoslovakia, Hungary, Romania, Bulgaria, East Germany and Albania. Part of the pact was an insistence that the countries of the pact still believed in the idea of the collective security of nations, i.e. that all nations of the world should unite to prevent any war. It was described as a Treaty of Friendship, Co-operation and Mutual Assistance between the countries who signed it. All the forces of the pact countries were placed under the leadership of a Soviet commander-in-chief and it permitted Soviet troops to be stationed in these countries for the purpose of defence. This became part of the USSR's methods of keeping the countries under its control and their troops would be used in the future to prevent Soviet satellite states from leaving Soviet control.

The Warsaw Pact was dominated by the USSR and was seen as a response to NATO. Although there was a thaw, Khrushchev was keen to ensure the safety of the communist states that surrounded Soviet Russia and the position of the USSR as their leader. He even strengthened this by visiting Yugoslavia and resuming friendly relations with President Tito. The formation of the Warsaw Pact meant that the division of Europe was now marked by two rival alliances. If there was a war, it would involve all the countries in NATO and the Warsaw Pact.

∞**links**

For more on Hungary, see pages 90–93.

For Czechoslovakia, look ahead to pages 110–113.

Activity

This activity could be completed as a discussion, debate or group activity.

1 a Which of the following contributed most to the development of the Cold War between 1949 and 1955?

    i   NATO and the Warsaw Pact

    ii The nuclear arms race

    iii The Korean War

    iv The death of Stalin

  b Which do you think was the main reason? Explain your answer.

Study tip

As in the previous activity, this is a possible stem for a bullet-point question. Don't forget that any of these bullet points could be paired with one from the previous activity.

Practice questions

Study **Source A** and then answer all three questions that follow.

Source A   President Truman explains his 'Doctrine'

> I believe that it must be the policy of the United States to support free people who are resisting attempted conquest by armed minorities or outside pressures. I believe that we must assist free peoples to work out their own destinies in their own way.

1   The Yalta Conference of February 1945 was a meeting of the leaders of the USSR, the USA and Britain to decide how to manage the peace once Germany had been defeated.

Describe the decisions that were agreed by the three leaders at Yalta.   *(4 marks)*

2   **Source A** suggests a reason why the Truman Doctrine was issued in March 1947.

Do you agree that this was the main reason for the Truman Doctrine?

Explain your answer by referring to the purpose of the source as well as using its content and your knowledge.   *(6 marks)*

3   Which was more important as a reason for the development of the Cold War in the years 1945 to 1955:

- Soviet expansion into Europe;
- the formation of NATO and the Warsaw Pact?

You must refer to **both** reasons when explaining your answer.   *(10 marks)*

5 Crises of the Cold War, 1955–70

5.1 How peaceful was 'peaceful co-existence'?

A U2 photos of the USSR building missile sites in Cuba, 1962

Objectives

In this chapter you will learn about:

the challenges to peaceful co-existence

the threats to Soviet control from Hungary and Czechoslovakia

international crises about spy planes, missiles and the Berlin Wall

the continuing arms and space race.

Khrushchev made his secret speech denouncing Stalin's brutality and stressing the need for peaceful co-existence with the West in February 1956. This change in Soviet policy did not stop the USSR violently crushing challenges to the Soviet control of communist Europe. It also did not put an end to crises between the superpowers which continued the Cold War. The rivalry between the USSR and USA continued and widened into space with the development of spacecraft and the implications that this had for security.

The Hungarian Rising

Background

Hungary had been treated as a defeated country by the Soviets after the Second World War and reparations had been taken from it. With the support of the USSR, a communist government had been established under Rakosi, who closely followed

Timeline

From peaceful co-existence to Czechoslovakia

Feb	1956	Khrushchev makes his secret speech
Nov	1956	Soviets crush Hungarian Rising
Oct	1957	USSR launches first satellite – Sputnik 1
Oct	1958	USA launches Pioneer 1 spacecraft
May	1960	U2 Crisis; Paris Summit Conference
Apr	1961	Soviets launch first man into space; Bay of Pigs invasion
May	1961	First American in space
Aug	1961	Berlin Wall built
Oct	1962	Cuban Missile Crisis
Oct	1963	Nuclear Test Ban Treaty
Aug	1968	Soviet troops invade Czechoslovakia; Brezhnev Doctrine
Jul	1969	USA lands first man on the moon

Stalin's rules and opposition was eliminated. When Stalin died, Rakosi was replaced by the more moderate Imre Nagy, but in 1955 Rakosi seized power again. Khrushchev's condemnation of Stalin and events in Poland in June 1956, where riots and disturbances had led to Khrushchev accepting a change of leader, encouraged the Hungarians to protest against Rakosi's leadership. The Hungarians hated Rakosi and his secret police (the AVH) because of the brutality they had shown, executing 2,000 opponents and imprisoning over 200,000. They were also protesting against the falling standard of living and increased poverty, which they blamed on Soviet policies. Many in Hungary saw this as the opportunity to end Soviet domination and improve relations with the West. This they felt would bring an improved economy and a higher standard of living.

Events

The protests increased and in October riots broke out in Budapest. Street fighting lasted for five days. Stalin's statue was pulled down and dragged through the streets, and prisoners were released. Only the security police, many of whom were hanged by rebels, remained loyal to the USSR. Rakosi was forced to resign and Soviet tanks moved in. The more popular Nagy became Prime Minister and the Soviet troops withdrew. The Hungarians celebrated what looked like a victory. It appeared that the USSR had been defeated by one of its satellites.

The new Hungarian government began to make reforms. These reforms would lead to free elections, the end of the secret police and the removal of the Soviet army of occupation. Khrushchev seemed to be accepting this. However, this changed when Nagy demanded the right for Hungary to withdraw from the Warsaw Pact and follow a neutral role in the Cold War. This was too much for the USSR. Free elections could mean the end of Communism in Hungary. If Hungary withdrew from the Warsaw Pact, there would be a gap in the Iron Curtain and the Soviet buffer zone with the West would be broken.

Key profile

Nikita Khrushchev

1894	Born 17 April, the son of a peasant family
1917	Joins and fights with the Red Army in the Civil War
1935	Becomes second-in-command in the Moscow Communist Party
1953	Shares power after the death of Stalin
1955	Supports peaceful co-existence with West
1956	Takes control in USSR – secret speech; sends tanks into Hungary
1960	Walks out of Paris Summit Meeting
1961	Builds Berlin Wall
1962	Places missiles on Cuba
1964	Forced from power
1971	Dies 11 September

Tasks

1   Why does Source **B** show the bears from Yugoslavia, Poland and Czechoslovakia leaving their bases?

2   Why did the Hungarians protest in Hungary in 1956?

B *Trainer Khrushchev's problems; a British cartoon of 31 October 1956*

Soviet control

Soviet troops re-entered Hungary on 1 November. By 4 November they had reached Budapest. Over 1,000 tanks moved into the city to crush the rising. Nagy appealed to the West for help but none came. The Soviets seized the radio station and there was no organised defence after 4 November. Two weeks of street fighting followed, but the Hungarians were no match for the Soviet forces and a new pro-Soviet communist government under Kadar was set up. Nagy was captured and promised a free passage out of Hungary but was later shot. Changes were made to avoid a repeat of the events, but Hungary was now firmly in Soviet control.

C Soviet tank disabled in Budapest

66 *This fight is the fight for freedom by the Hungarian people against the Russian intervention ... Russian armed forces, contrary to all treaties and conventions, are crushing the resistance of the Hungarian people ... This is the most brutal form of intervention. I ask that the revolutionary leaders should turn to all the peoples of the world for help and explain that today it is Hungary and tomorrow, or the day after tomorrow, it will be the turn of other countries because the imperialism of Moscow does not know borders.* 99

D Part of Nagy's broadcast, 4 November 1956

> 66 *We must put an end to the excesses of the counter-revolutionary elements. The hour for action has sounded. We are going to defend the interest of the workers and peasants and the achievements of the people's democracy. Let all the faithful fighters of the true cause of* **socialism** *come out of hiding and take up arms.* 99

E *Extract from Kadar's statement on setting up the Hungarian Revolutionary Worker– Peasant government in opposition to Nagy, 4 November 1956*

Key terms

Socialism: Kadar was referring to Communism when he used this word.

Patriots: people who are prepared to defend the rights and freedoms of their own country.

Results

The USSR claimed that it had gone into Hungary to support Kadar and Hungarian **patriots**, who had formed a government of revolutionary workers to oppose Nagy. The Soviets claimed they were forced to do this because the government of Nagy had allowed itself to be dominated by a fascist mob, financed by the imperialist West. When the UN looked into the details of the rising, it found no evidence of popular support in Hungary for Kadar's new government.

The results of the rising for Europe and the Cold War were as follows:

■ Between 2,500 and 30,000 Hungarians, mostly civilians, were killed along with 700 Soviet troops.

■ Over 200,000 refugees fled Hungary and settled in the West.

■ There was no active support for the rising in the West – the Americans simply protested.

■ Other satellite states in Eastern Europe did not dare to challenge Soviet authority after Hungary.

■ Khrushchev strengthened his position in the USSR and showed the West that peaceful co-existence had its limits.

■ It marked a stalemate in the Cold War – the West did not interfere with Soviet activities in Eastern Europe.

Tasks

3   Study Sources **D** and **E**.

a   Explain the meaning of Source **D**.

b   How does Source **E** differ from Source **D**?

c   Why do you think the two sources differ? Explain your answer.

4   What reasons did the USSR give for its intervention on 4 November?

5   Explain what you can learn from Source **C** about the Hungarian Rising of 1956.

6   What effect did the Hungarian Rising have on the Cold War?

7   Explain why the West did not help Hungary in 1956.

Study tip

'Describe' questions can be set on Hungary 1956 and it can also be part of a bullet point question, e.g. the part the Hungarian Rising played in the development of the Cold War or how the events of the Rising illustrate Khrushchev's idea of 'peaceful co-existence'.

The beginning of the space race

Timeline
Nuclear arms and the space race

Oct	**1957**	USSR launches first satellite – Sputnik 1
Nov	**1957**	USSR puts a dog into space on Sputnik 2
Jan	**1958**	USA launches satellite – Explorer 1
Sep	**1959**	Soviet satellite Luna 2 reaches the moon
Oct	**1959**	Soviets picture the other side of the moon using Luna 3
Apr	**1961**	Soviets send first man, Yuri Gagarin, into space on Vostok 1
May	**1961**	Alan Shepherd becomes first American in space aboard Mercury Freedom 7
Feb	**1962**	John Glenn orbits the earth
Dec	**1962**	USA sends rocket to Venus – Mariner 2
Jun	**1963**	Soviet Valentina Tereshkova becomes first woman in space
Mar	**1965**	Alexei Leonov (USSR) makes first space walk – Voskhod 2
Jun	**1965**	Ed White makes first American space walk – Gemini 4
Apr	**1967**	Soyuz 1 (USSR) crash lands – first space flight fatality
Jul	**1969**	Neil Armstrong becomes first man on the moon
Jan	**1971**	First US exploration of the moon – Apollo 14
	1972	End of American moon landing programme

F *Valentina Tereshkova, 1963*

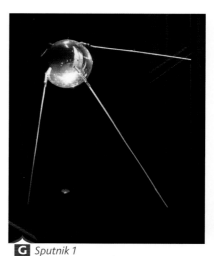

G *Sputnik 1*

H *American astronauts on the moon – Apollo 14, January 1971*

❝ *The US now sleeps under a Soviet moon.* ❞

I *Nikita Khrushchev speaking in 1957 after the launch of Sputnik 1*

The timeline shows that the USSR developed the technology to fire a satellite into space before the USA. This not only upset the pride of the Americans as they considered that they were superior to communist countries, it also affected their security. This was because the space race was closely tied in with the development of nuclear weapons and the nuclear arms race. There was a fear that every crisis in this period could result in a nuclear war.

The continuation of the nuclear arms race

Up to 1957, the USA were always ahead in the development of nuclear weapons. The launch of Sputnik 1 in 1957 changed this. The USSR was America's main enemy in the 1950s. To use nuclear weapons against the Soviets, the USA would have to carry them in aeroplanes, which could easily be shot down. The launch of the Sputnik meant that the Soviets had developed rockets which could carry nuclear warheads and reach the USA. The USA developed its own Intercontinental Ballistic Missiles (ICBMs) in 1957 and, by 1959, they could be stored underground and ready for use in 30 seconds. The firing of a Polaris missile from a nuclear submarine by the USA in 1960 meant that a missile could be fired from the sea closer to the USSR and therefore be more accurate. ICBMs were placed in friendly powers close to America's enemy. The USA placed missiles in Turkey in 1959 and the USSR tried to place them in Cuba in 1962.

In the 1960s both superpowers were intent on having enough nuclear weapons to be able to respond to an attack. They kept a check on the progress being made by the other power by a series of spy networks. Each superpower possessed enough weapons to destroy the other and therefore they were less likely to use them. They had to continue to build up these weapons to keep the balance, which was expensive but prevented war. This was known as the 'nuclear deterrent'. By the end of the 1960s the superpowers had enough nuclear weapons to destroy the rest of the world. This became known as Mutually Assured Destruction (MAD). The arms and space race may have prevented war, but they were extremely expensive.

Did you know ??????

The *James Bond* books were written by Ian Fleming during the Cold War and first made into films in the 1960s.

∞ links

See page 83 for the nuclear arms race.

See pages 104–109 for the Cuban Missile Crisis.

J *Strategic nuclear missiles' warheads of USA and USSR, 1964–70*

	Launchers		Warheads		Megatonnage	
Year	USA	USSR	USA	USSR	USA	USSR
1964	2,416	375	6,800	500	7,500	1,000
1966	2,396	435	5,000	550	5,600	1,200
1968	2,360	1,045	4,500	850	5,100	2,300
1970	2,230	1,680	3,900	1,800	4,300	3,100

Tasks

8   The Soviets considered that the launch of Sputnik 1 was a great victory for them in the Cold War. Explain why.

9   Why do you think the USSR designed the stamp in Source **F**?

10   What did Khrushchev mean in Source **I**?

11   Had anyone won the space race and nuclear arms race by 1970? Use the Key chronology on page 94 and Source **J** as well as the text to explain your answer.

The U2 Crisis

As part of his policy of peaceful co-existence, Khrushchev had visited the USA in 1959 and it was agreed to hold a Summit Meeting of the leaders of the USSR, USA, Britain and France in 1960. The meeting was to be held in Paris and its purpose would be to solve some of the Cold War problems. There were high hopes that the USSR would sign a peace treaty with Germany and there would be an end to the Cold War. These hopes were shattered when, just before the Summit Meeting was due to start, an American U2 plane was shot down over the USSR.

The U2 was a spy plane developed by the Americans. It could fly at high altitudes, out of the range of most planes. The Americans had been using them successfully for four years to spy on the Soviets. On 1 May 1960, an American pilot, Gary Powers, took off from a US air base in Pakistan and flew over the USSR, taking photos of military sites in the USSR for the **CIA**. The first part of the flight was successful, but then the U2 was hit by a Soviet missile near the town of Sverdlovsk. Powers was forced to eject from the plane and was captured by the Soviets. The plane was recovered and the photos developed, so Khrushchev now knew that Powers had been on a spying mission.

Key terms

CIA: short for 'Central Intelligence Agency', this is the American civilian body that collects information about foreign governments to aid American decision-making.

K *A Lockheed Martin U2 spy plane*

At first, Khrushchev simply announced that an American plane had been shot down over the USSR. The Americans immediately began to try to cover up the truth. They announced that one of their weather planes had gone missing over Turkey and must have gone off course. The Americans did not know that Powers had been captured and that he had admitted to spying. Moreover, the Soviets had the proof: the photos that had been found on the U2. Khrushchev announced this to the world, demanding an apology from the USA and a promise to stop any future flights and to punish those responsible. The Americans had been caught spying and lying about it, but Eisenhower, the American President, refused to apologise. Eisenhower claimed that the USA had to use spying missions to protect itself. Khrushchev condemned the American response, stormed out of the Summit Meeting and withdrew his invitation to Eisenhower to visit the USSR. The Paris Summit and the thaw in relations between the superpowers were at an end.

Gary Powers was accused of spying and put on trial in the USSR. He was found guilty and sentenced to 10 years imprisonment. After serving part of his sentence, he was released in 1962 in exchange for a top Soviet spy who had been captured by the Americans.

> **Did you know ??????**
>
> Eisenhower was President of the United States from 1953–1961. His presidency was notable for several reasons: he contributed to the cease-fire of the Korean war, made nuclear weapons a higher defence priority and launched the Space Race.

L *The trial of Gary Powers*

Tasks

12 Why did the USA use spy planes in 1960?

13 Explain how Khrushchev tricked Eisenhower in the U2 Crisis of 1960.

14 What can you learn from Source **L** about the trial of Gary Powers?

15 What was the most important result of the U2 Crisis for the following?

  a The world

  b The USA

  c The USSR

The importance of the U2 Crisis

- It ended the Paris Summit Meeting and the progress towards a solution to the Cold War. This meant that there was no Test Ban Treaty and the problem of Berlin remained, which led to the building of the Berlin Wall.
- Peaceful co-existence was at an end.
- Eisenhower and the Americans were blamed for the failure. In the presidential election at the end of 1960, Eisenhower's Vice President, Richard Nixon, was defeated by the democrat John F. Kennedy.
- It was a propaganda victory for Khrushchev and the USSR.
- America placed its forces on alert as it expected some form of retaliation from the USSR. The mistrust created by the U2 Crisis was partly responsible for the Cuban Missile Crisis of 1962.
- Although Eisenhower had promised an end to all American spying missions, it led to an acceleration of work in the USA on new methods and systems for spying.
- The Chinese felt that it proved their belief that the USA could not be trusted, so peaceful co-existence would never work.

∞links

See pages 100–109 for details on the Berlin Wall and Cuban Missile Crisis.

Key terms

Espionage: spying – the use of secret agents to collect information, normally of a military nature.

> " On May 1 a US military reconnaissance aircraft invaded the Soviet Union while executing a specific **espionage** mission to obtain information on military and industrial installations on the territory of the USSR ... the aircraft was shot down by units of the Soviet rocket forces. If the US government is really ready to co-operate with the governments of the other powers in the interests of maintaining peace, it must first condemn the provocative actions of the US air force with regard to the Soviet Union; and secondly, prevent ... such a policy against the Soviet Union continuing in the future ... Until this is done, the Soviet government sees no possibility for fruitful negotiations with the US government at the summit conference. "

M Extract from Khrushchev's statement on the U2 Crisis, 16 May 1960

> " The position of the United States was made clear with respect to the distasteful necessity of espionage activities in a world where nations distrust each other's intentions ... these activities had no aggressive intent but rather were to assure the safety of the United States and the free world against surprise attack by a power which boasts of its ability to devastate the USA and other countries by missiles. These flights were suspended ... and are not to be resumed. I have come to Paris to seek agreements with the Soviet Union which would eliminate the need for all forms of espionage. Mr Khrushchev ... came all the way from Moscow to Paris with the sole intention of sabotaging this meeting on which so much of the hopes of the world have rested. "

N Extract from Eisenhower's reply, 16 May 1960

O *British cartoon of the U2 Crisis, 1960. The characters on the left are De Gaulle (President of France), Eisenhower and Macmillan (British Prime Minister). Khrushchev is on the right of the hill*

Tasks

16 Why do you think the USSR put Gary Powers on trial? Use Source **L** to help you.

17 Explain the meaning of Source **M**.

18 What was Eisenhower trying to do in his reply in Source **N**?

19 In Source **O**, what do you think the following are meant to represent?
  a The plane
  b The bird
  c The hill

20 What is the message of the cartoon in Source **O**?

Activity

This activity could be completed as a discussion, debate or group activity.

1 Re-enact an argument between Khrushchev and Eisenhower about the reasons for the failure of the Paris Summit Meeting. What evidence would Khrushchev use to support him and what factors would Eisenhower use?

The Berlin Wall

The position of Berlin as a divided city in the Soviet sector of Germany made it a centre of rivalry between East and West. Stalin's attempt to gain control of West Berlin in 1948–49 had been defeated by the Berlin Airlift. Khrushchev had also demanded that the West gave up West Berlin in 1958, but backed down when he realised that the Americans would oppose any attempted takeover. The Marshall Plan meant that living standards in West Berlin were much better than in the East. West Berlin was an advert for capitalism. The people there were able to buy luxury goods whereas those in East Berlin were much poorer. Many reacted to this by crossing the border and living in the West. Over 2 million people defected from East to West Berlin between 1945 and 1961. Many of these were educated people and skilled workers whom the East could ill afford to lose. This was a severe embarrassment to Khrushchev and to Communism. In 1961 he decided to put a stop to this movement of citizens.

When the new American President, John F. Kennedy, refused to give up West Berlin in 1961, Khrushchev decided to close the border. Overnight on 13 August 1961 the city was cut into two by barbed wire and the crossing points were either sealed or guarded with Soviet tanks. The USA took little action about this other than to issue a protest. Kennedy sent his Vice President, Lyndon B. Johnson, to Berlin with some additional troops. All this did was restore West German morale and make the Soviets realise that the USA would resist any attempt to extend communist influence into West Berlin. There was a small confrontation of tanks at the main crossing point, Checkpoint Charlie, in October which could have escalated, but no shots were fired and the tanks withdrew.

∞links

See the Potsdam Conference on page 72 and the Berlin Blockade on page 79 for details of the division of Germany and Berlin.

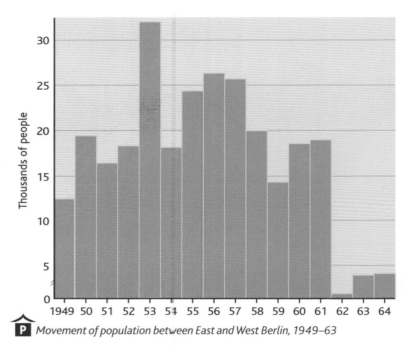

P Movement of population between East and West Berlin, 1949–63

The wall goes up

The barbed wire was soon replaced by a massive stone wall 45 km long and about 3.6 m wide. It was built slightly inside the borders of East Germany so that there was no attempt to extend the boundary into West Berlin. Throughout the building process, soldiers guarded the border with orders to kill anyone who attempted to defect to West

Task

21 Study Source **P**.

a What does this graph tell you about the effect of the Berlin Wall?

b Does this help us to explain why the wall was built? Explain your answer.

Berlin. The Berlin Wall completely sealed off the boundary between East and West Berlin. Families and friends were separated. Around 60,000 commuters who had travelled daily from East to West Berlin for work were no longer allowed to travel to West Berlin.

Anyone trying to cross the wall was shot. More than 40 Germans were killed trying to cross into West Berlin in the first year of the wall. Others managed to avoid the guards and escape to the West, normally by climbing the wall in the early days, though later, when the defences of the wall were strengthened, tunnels were used and more inventive methods of escape were devised, one of which involved using a hot air balloon. Eventually, eight border crossings were set up, one of which was Checkpoint Charlie. Visits from West Germany to East Berlin were allowed, but only if you obtained a permit. It was far more difficult to get a permit if you wanted to travel from East to West Berlin.

Its main achievement for the USSR was that it reduced the number of defectors. The West accepted the wall with just a protest, but their governments made full propaganda use of the wall. They claimed that it was a failure for Communism because the USSR had to cage in their citizens to prevent them escaping.

Q *The stand-off of tanks at Checkpoint Charlie, 1961*

Did you know ??????

Some apartment buildings made up sections of the Berlin Wall. Initially, people could enter one of these buildings and walk straight out the back door or window into West Berlin. Soon all exits on the lower floors were bricked up, so then people began jumping from second- and third-story windows, onto blankets being held by West Berliners below. Later all these escape routes were bricked over.

One of the most dramatic deaths was that of Peter Fechter, in 1962. He was shot by border guards and left to bleed to death in broad daylight.

Tasks

22 Describe what is happening in Source **Q**.

23 Explain why the situation was dangerous.

Views of the Wall

In 1963 Kennedy visited the wall and made a speech in which he stated that to be a citizen of Berlin was the proudest boast of a free man. The speech was greeted with loud cheering by the people of West Berlin.

> **"** The Western powers in Berlin use it as a centre of subversive activity against East Germany. In no other part of the world are so many spy centres to be found. These centres smuggle their agents into East Germany for all kinds of subversion: recruiting spies; sabotage; provoking disturbances. The government will block this subversive activity and establish reliable safeguards and effective control around West Berlin, including its border with democratic Berlin. **"**

R *The Soviet government's reasons for building the Berlin Wall, 1961*

> **"** The crisis is over. If the Russians wanted to attack us and cut off the access routes, they wouldn't be putting up barbed wire borders. I am not going to get annoyed about it. **"**

S *President Kennedy commenting on the Berlin Wall, 1961*

> **"** As a free man I take pride in the words: Ich bin ein Berliner ['I am a citizen of Berlin']. **"**

T *President Kennedy speaking at the wall, June 1963*

U *The Berlin Wall: families divided. A daughter talks to her mother over the wall, 1961*

Tasks

24 List all the actions taken by President Kennedy between 1961 and 1963 to oppose the USSR in Berlin.

25 Do you think his opposition was successful? Explain your answer.

The importance of the Berlin Wall

- It reduced the number of defections from East Berlin. There were around 5,000 successful escapes from East Berlin after the wall compared to over 3 million in the years before the wall.
- It ended up as a propaganda victory for the Americans. The shooting of people attempting to defect added to this as the Americans criticised the tyranny of the communist rule, which had to use walls and force to stop its citizens from escaping.
- It stabilised the economy of East Germany – only one currency existed. The economy of East Germany certainly grew after the building of the wall and the government of East Germany gained greater control of its citizens.
- It was settled peacefully: Kennedy's reaction showed that he did not want to lose face, but he did not want to go to war over Berlin. He successfully overcame criticism from those in West Germany who wanted him to react in an aggressive manner.
- Plans for a united Berlin and Germany were ended. The USA no longer feared a repeat of the Berlin Blockade of 1948. The USSR had clearly given up all hope of taking control of West Berlin.
- It removed a likely area of conflict between the superpowers. Berlin had been a problem area between the superpowers since it was divided and they had almost come to blows over it in 1948–49 over the Berlin Blockade and Airlift.
- The official number of deaths attempting to cross the wall was 136. Some say that it could have been as many as 200.

Tasks

26 Read Source **R**.

  a What reasons for building the Berlin Wall are given in Source **R**?

  b Can you trust this source? Explain your answer.

27 Read Source **S**.

  a How does this source explain the USA's actions over the building of the Berlin Wall?

  b Why do you think President Kennedy made the statement in Source **T**? What did he mean?

28 What can you learn about the Berlin Wall from Sources **Q** and **U**?

⊂⊃ **links**

See Source **P** on page 100 for more on defections.

Activity

This activity could be completed as a discussion, debate or group activity.

2 Which country do you think gained more from the building of the Berlin Wall:

  a the USSR;

  b the USA?

⊂⊃ **links**

Turn back to pages 79–81 for the Berlin Blockade and Airlift.

Key profile

John F. Kennedy

1917	Born 29 May in the USA of Irish descent
1940	Joins the navy; fights and is wounded in the Second World War
1947	Enters Congress
1960	Elected President of the USA – the first Roman Catholic to hold the office
1961	Supports Cuban rebels at the Bay of Pigs
1962	Cuban Missile Crisis
1963	Assassinated in Dallas

How close to war was the world in the 1960s?

■ The Cuban Missile Crisis

Castro and Cuba

Cuba is an island about 160 km from the American mainland. Until 1959 it was ruled by the corrupt dictator Batista, who was friendly with the USA. American businessmen owned property and industry in Cuba and the USA was a major market for Cuban goods. In 1959 Batista was overthrown in a revolution led by Fidel Castro. Castro became leader of Cuba and wanted to get rid of all foreign influence in the country. He seized all the land owned by Americans and nationalised American businesses. In retaliation, the USA refused to buy the Cubans' main export, sugar cane, so Castro arranged to sell it to the USSR. The Americans became extremely concerned about Cuba. Castro was believed to be a communist and the USA feared any expansion of Communism. Moreover, the USSR now had an ally close to the USA.

The Bay of Pigs

Before Kennedy came to power, there was a plan to invade Cuba and link up with the opponents of Castro on the island. Kennedy was advised by the CIA that Castro could be overthrown if the USA supported a group of Cuban rebels. With American support, a force of around 1,400 rebels landed at the Bay of Pigs in Cuba. They were trapped on the beach by Castro's forces and unable to link up with rebels on the island. As a result, they were easily defeated by Castro's forces.

This was a disaster for Kennedy. Many in the USA blamed him because he had refused to give air cover to the invasion as he did not want to be seen to be openly supporting the rebels. The sympathy of the world was with Cuba, not the Americans. To make matters worse, the Americans still had a naval base at Guantanamo in Cuba and Castro feared that they would attack Cuba again, so he turned to the USSR for help. He announced he was a communist and Khrushchev began to provide him with weapons and surface-to-air missiles (SAMs) that would be able to shoot down any attacking American planes. Moreover, Kennedy's action made Khrushchev think Kennedy was weak, so Krushchev tried to take advantage of this by supplying Cuba with long-range missiles that could be fired at the USA.

The start of the Cuban Missile Crisis

As the Soviets had not yet developed missiles like Polaris, which could be fired from submarines, a base in Cuba – so close to the USA – would enable them to threaten the Americans. Khrushchev saw the missile bases in Cuba as an answer to the American bases in Turkey. The USA suspected that these missile bases were being set up but, when challenged, Khrushchev denied it and claimed that the USSR had no intention of placing missiles on Cuba.

> **Study tip**
>
> The Bay of Pigs invasion and the Cuban Missile Crisis are two separate events. However, the Bay of Pigs helped to bring about the Cuban Missile Crisis.

Then, on 16 October 1962, an American U2 spy plane took photos of launch pads that were being built for long-range missiles on Cuba. At this stage, there were no missiles but, when in place, they could carry hydrogen bombs and could reach and destroy most cities in the USA within 20 minutes. Millions of American lives would be lost in such an attack. Kennedy had to take some action to prevent this.

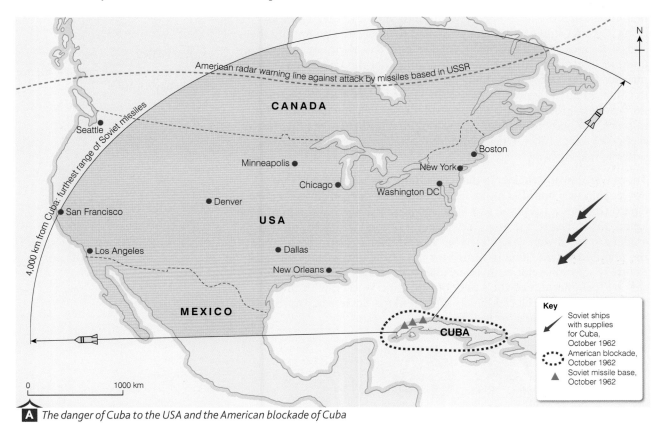

A *The danger of Cuba to the USA and the American blockade of Cuba*

The difficulties facing the USA

Kennedy was faced with a difficult decision. If he ignored the missiles on Cuba and simply made a diplomatic protest as he had done over the Berlin Wall, it would appear that he had backed down and was weak. If he launched an attack on Cuba to remove the missile bases, it would involve loss of life. If it was a nuclear attack it could provoke a nuclear war with the USSR and result in the destruction of much of the world. Soviet ships with missiles on board were heading for Cuba. Kennedy decided that the best course of action was to put a naval blockade around Cuba. On 22 October he announced that the sea within 800 km of Cuba would be placed in **quarantine** and that no ships carrying weapons would be allowed through by the US navy. Kennedy called on Khrushchev to withdraw the weapons from Cuba.

Key terms

Quarantine: a period of isolation.

Crisis point

Soviet ships carrying rockets approached Cuba. The world held its breath; the Soviet ships would soon reach the American blockade. On 24 October, when in sight of the blockade, the ships turned round. The immediate danger of a clash between the two superpowers had been prevented, but the Cuban Missile Crisis was not over. Kennedy demanded that the Soviets remove all their sites and missiles from Cuba. On 26 October Khrushchev agreed to consider dismantling the sites if Kennedy lifted the blockade. The next day, Kennedy received another letter from Khrushchev demanding that the USA remove its missiles from Turkey in exchange for the Soviet removal of missiles in Cuba. Kennedy ignored this second letter and replied to the one of 26 October agreeing to lift the blockade if Khrushchev dismantled the missiles. Kennedy threatened to invade Cuba if Khrushchev had not replied by 29 October. Once again, the world was on the brink of a possible nuclear war.

There were several incidents that could have provoked a war. One Soviet ship was boarded and a crate containing nuclear bombs opened. On 26 October a U2 plane was shot down over Cuba and the pilot was killed. Mr U. Thant, the Secretary General of the UN, urged the two leaders to avoid war. On 28 October Khrushchev agreed to dismantle the missile sites on Cuba in return for the lifting of the blockade and Kennedy's promise not to invade Cuba. Khrushchev was able to claim that he had guaranteed the safety of Cuba and worked with the UN to prevent war. The blockade was lifted and the Soviets began to dismantle the missile sites in Cuba.

links

See Sources **E** and **F** on page 108 for Krushchev's letters.

B *The heads of Khrushchev and Kennedy blowing away the wrecked ship of Cuba*

> 66 *To halt this offensive build-up, a strict quarantine on all offensive military equipment under shipment to Cuba is being initiated. All ships of any kind bound for Cuba from whatever nation and port will, if found to contain cargoes of offensive weapons, be turned back. This quarantine will be extended, if needed, to other types of cargo and carriers. We are not at this time, however, denying the necessities of life as the Soviets attempted to do in their Berlin Blockade of 1948.* 99

C *President Kennedy's televised speech, 22 October*

> 66 *The Soviet government considers the violation of the freedom of navigation in international waters and air space to constitute an act of aggression propelling humankind into the abyss of a world nuclear-missile war. Therefore, the Soviet government cannot instruct captains of Soviet ships bound for Cuba to observe orders of American naval forces blockading this island. Our instructions to Soviet sailors are to observe strictly the generally accepted standards of navigation in international waters and not retreat one step from them. And, if the American side violates these rights, it must be aware of the responsibility it will bear for this act.* 99

D *Khrushchev's reply to the quarantine*

The results of the Cuban Missile Crisis

- Nuclear war had been avoided, to the relief of the whole world. The Cuban Missile Crisis is normally regarded as the nearest that the world has ever been to nuclear war and mass destruction. It was the most tense moment of the Cold War.
- The Soviets now had a communist ally near the USA, which started to balance out the allies that the USA had near to the USSR.
- Kennedy's reputation was increased: he was seen as strong because he had stood up to Khrushchev and forced him to back down over the missiles. It restored his prestige after the failure of the Bay of Pigs invasion.
- Khrushchev had successfully protected Cuba and claimed that he was the peacemaker who had listened to the appeal of the UN to avoid war and seek peace.
- Both leaders understood how close they had come to war and realised that this was due to their policies of **brinkmanship**. This led to a thaw in the tension of the Cold War. A telephone link between Washington and Moscow ('the hotline') was set up so the leaders of the two superpowers could talk to each other directly. A Disarmament Conference was held in 1962, which resulted in the signing of a Nuclear Test Ban Treaty that banned the testing of nuclear weapons in the air or on the ground to avoid polluting the atmosphere. They could still be tested underground.
- Although Kennedy had refused to withdraw American missiles in Turkey because it would cause a division in NATO, he secretly agreed that he would withdraw them a few months later.

 links

See page 79 for the Berlin Blockade.

Did you know ??????

The Cuban Missile Crisis lasted over two weeks. Throughout that time, there was a real fear in the world that nuclear war would break out.

Key terms

Brinkmanship: a policy of risking war to achieve your aims – pushing the other power to the edge.

Did you know ??????

When the Americans withdrew their missiles from Turkey, the Soviets claimed it as a victory; the Americans claimed that they had withdrawn the weapons because they were out of date.

> 66 *If the President of the United States assures us that the USA will not take part in any attacks on Cuba, and lift the blockade of that island, then the question of the removal of the missile sites would follow. I propose to send no more missiles to Cuba and to withdraw or destroy those weapons within Cuba as long as you promise to end the blockade and agree not to invade Cuba.* 99

E *Extract from letter sent by Khrushchev to Kennedy, 26 October 1962*

> 66 *You are worried over Cuba because it lies ninety miles across the sea from the shores of the United States. Turkey lies next to us. You have placed rocket weapons in Turkey right next to us. This is why I make this proposal: we agree to remove the weapons from Cuba on condition that the United States withdraws its similar weapons from Turkey.* 99

F *Extract from letter sent by Khrushchev to Kennedy, 27 October 1962*

> 66 *I was in the university library when I first heard of the American blockade of Cuba. Everyone was talking about it, in the coffee bars, in the students' union and in between all lectures. Even the lecturers were discussing it as part of the lecture! What would happen? Would it mean the end of the world? Special services held in churches were full. Everyone felt helpless. What a relief it was when the Crisis was over. We all went out and celebrated the survival of the world.* 99

G *British university student, who was 19 in 1962, remembers Cuba in 2008*

Task

1 Read Sources **E** and **F**. Kennedy received these letters on two consecutive days.

a Explain the main difference between the sources.

b How do you think Kennedy would feel after he had received the first letter?

c How would this have changed when he received the second letter?

d Why do you think Khrushchev sent the second letter?

e What action did Kennedy take?

f Was this a risk?

g Did it work? Explain your answer.

H *Khrushchev and Kennedy arm wrestling, a British cartoon published in 1962*

Tasks

2 Using information from the text and sources, draw a timeline of the events in the Cuban Missile Crisis. Begin with 16 October and continue until 31 October.

3 When was the crisis at its most serious? Explain your answer.

4 Why were Soviet missiles on Cuba such a danger to the USA? Use Source **A** on page 105 to explain your answer.

5 Study Source **C** on page 107.
  a What does the source mean?
  b How is President Kennedy trying to justify the American blockade?
  c Why do you think he made this speech on television?

6 Study Source **D** on page 107.
  a Explain Khrushchev's argument in the source.
  b Explain the meaning of the orders that Khrushchev gave to his ships.
  c What would have happened if these orders had not been changed?

7 What can you learn about the feeling in Britain at the time of the Cuban Missile Crisis from Source **G**? Explain your answer.

8 Explain the meaning of Source **H**.

9 How reliable are Sources **G** and **H**? Explain your answer.

10 The USA had been involved in a war in Korea in 1950–53, which also involved China. Why do you think the Cuban Missile Crisis is regarded as a greater danger to the world than this war? Explain your answer.

⃝⃝ links

See pages 84–87 for more on the Korean War.

Activities

These activities could be completed as a discussion, debate or group activity.

1 Khrushchev claimed that he was the peacemaker in the Cuban Missile Crisis. Find evidence that supports this claim. Do you think the Americans would agree with Khrushchev's version? Explain why, supporting your view with evidence.

2 Both the USA and the USSR claimed victory in the Cuban Crisis. Find the evidence that supports the claims for a Soviet victory and that which supports an American victory. What is your conclusion? Who was the more successful in the Cuban Missile Crisis?

Czechoslovakia

Czechoslovakia was the last of the satellite states to become communist in 1948. It had applied for Marshall Aid from the USA but Stalin prevented this. From 1948 until 1968 it was ruled by Novotny, who was loyal to the USSR. Czechoslovakia had been a democracy from 1919 to 1938 and objected to the control that the Soviets placed on it. The Czechs wanted more freedom in their lives and wider trade. In January 1968 Novotny was forced to resign and was replaced by Alexander Dubcek.

The Prague Spring

As leader of the Czech Communist Party, Dubcek believed in Communism but introduced a more relaxed version – or, as he called it, 'Communism with a human face'. He believed that the government should respond to the needs of the people. Censorship of the press and radio was removed and the powers of the secret police reduced. Government control of industry and agriculture was reduced and trade unions were given greater powers. The borders with the West were opened: Czechs were permitted to trade with the West and travel there. Dubcek remembered what had happened in Hungary in 1956 and constantly stressed to the Soviets that Czechoslovakia was still communist and that he had no intention of withdrawing from the Warsaw Pact. The reforms, known as the Prague Spring, were popular in Czechoslovakia but caused some concern in the USSR.

I A street cartoon in Czechoslovakia, August 1968. It shows Lenin, the founder of Communism, weeping at the presence of Soviet troops in Czechoslovakia

Task

11 Explain the meaning of Source I.

The USSR's response

The Soviet leader, Brezhnev, was worried that the introduction of free speech in Czechoslovakia would lead to demands for more freedom in the USSR and its satellite countries. Opposition to Czechoslovakia was encouraged by Warsaw Pact leaders. Communist leaders in the satellite countries thought that increased freedom in Czechoslovakia would weaken their position in their own countries. Brezhnev was concerned that Czechoslovakia would look more to the West than to the USSR and, in this way, cause a gap in the Iron Curtain which could lead to its collapse.

Brezhnev tried to negotiate. Dubcek was consulted and the position of Czechoslovakia was discussed by all the Warsaw Pact countries. Dubcek constantly maintained that Czechoslovakia was still communist and would remain within the Warsaw Pact. It was a great surprise to him and the rest of the world when on 20 August 1968 Soviet tanks and troops from the Warsaw Pact countries invaded Czechoslovakia.

Remembering what had happened in Hungary in 1956, the Czech government did not resist, so there was no fighting, only passive resistance by the people of Czechoslovakia – fewer than 100 people were killed in the invasion. There were demonstrations against the invaders and some Soviet tanks were attacked with homemade bombs or covered in whitewash. Street cartoons appeared criticising the Soviet invasion. The Soviet troops were surprised by how much the Czech people hated them because of their presence in Czechoslovakia. Dubcek was recalled to Moscow and replaced by Husak. The reforms of the Prague Spring were withdrawn. Opposition continued and a student, Jan Palach, set himself on fire in Prague in January 1969 in protest at the removal of Czech freedoms. Dubcek was allowed to return as a minor official, but eventually he was dismissed from the Communist Party. After about a year, the opposition died down; the Soviets had restored their control by force.

> 66 *Yesterday troops of the Warsaw Pact countries crossed the frontiers of the Czechoslovak Socialist Republic. This happened without the knowledge of the Czech government. The Czechoslovak communist party appeals to all our citizens to maintain calm and not to offer any resistance. Our army has not received the command to defend the country. The Czechoslovak communist party regards this act of invasion as being against the principles of the socialist states and of international law.* 99

 J *Broadcast by Czech Communist Party on Prague Radio, 21 August 1968*

∞ **links**

For the Hungarian Rising, see pages 90–93.

Task

12 Explain the meaning of Source **J**.

a Do Sources **I** and **L** indicate that the broadcast was obeyed by the Czech people?

b What can you learn about the feelings of the Czech people in 1968 from Sources **I** and **L**?

> *Party and government leaders of Czechoslovakia have asked the Soviet Union and other allied states to give brotherly help with the armed forces. This request was caused by the threat from counter-revolutionary forces. The actions do not attack the interests of any country. They serve the purpose of peace. The brotherly countries are resisting any threat from outside. Nobody will ever be allowed to break a single link from the chain of Socialist countries.*

K *Soviet statement issued by the press agency Tass, 21 August 1968*

Tasks

13 How does Source **K** differ from Source **J**?

14 How accurate do you think Source **K** is on the reasons for the Soviet intervention in Czechoslovakia? Explain your answer.

Hint

For Task 14, remember to examine the provenance of the source as well as testing its accuracy using your knowledge.

L *Opposition to the Soviet invasion of Czechoslovakia*

> **"** *Wednesday 21 August: The sound of jets screaming overhead woke me just after 2am. The thought of a Russian invasion crossed my mind, but it seemed too melodramatic after all that had happened in the last few weeks, so I assumed it was a military exercise. After breakfast, I went to the top of the building to get a better view of what was going on. I saw a convoy of motor scooters and several lorries with Czech flags crowded with young people shouting 'Dubcek! Dubcek!' We heard that there were tanks all round the Old Town Square and that young Czechs were deliberately blocking the movement of the tanks. Some surrounded the soldiers and tank crews and tried to explain the truth to young Russian soldiers who obviously had no idea of the true nature of their mission. Some of them thought they were on a military exercise.* **"**

M Excerpts from the diary of Gordon Paton. Gordon was staying with his family in the British Embassy in Prague during the school holidays in August 1968. He was the son-in-law of Sir William Barker, who was the British Ambassador to Prague

Tasks

Read Source **M**.

15 What does this source tell us about the following?

  a The nature of the invasion

  b The attitude of the Czechs to the invasion

  c The attitude of the Russian soldiers

16 How reliable do you think this source is? Explain your answer.

The Brezhnev Doctrine

The Brezhnev Doctrine was the name given to the statement to explain Soviet intervention in Czechoslovakia. The Soviet leader, Brezhnev, made it policy in a speech in November 1968. He said:

> **"** *When forces that are hostile to socialism try to turn the development of some Socialist country towards capitalism, it becomes not only a problem of the country concerned, but a common problem and concern of all Socialist countries.* **"**

N The Brezhnev Doctrine

This speech made it clear that any country which attempted to break away from Soviet control would be regarded as a threat to the whole of the Warsaw Pact countries. This put an end to any hopes of reforming Communism. The Brezhnev Doctrine remained in force until it was reversed by President Gorbachev in 1989.

The effects of events in Czechoslovakia

- The suppression of Dubcek's reforms and the Brezhnev Doctrine sent a clear signal to the rest of the satellite countries that the USSR would resist any attempt to break away from Soviet-controlled communist countries.

links

See page 125 for more on President Gorbachev.

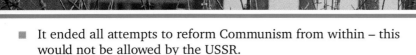

- It ended all attempts to reform Communism from within – this would not be allowed by the USSR.

- The Czechs became even more resentful of Soviet rule, but realised that there was little they could do about it. Over 250,000 emigrated in the years after 1968.

- The West disapproved of the Soviet action, but did nothing. Relations had been better with the USSR since Cuba and the USA realised that any action on behalf of Czechoslovakia would ruin this. It was another example of the USSR being allowed to control its area of influence without interference. The invasion of Czechoslovakia was no threat to the security of the USA or any NATO country, so the USSR was left to get on with it.

Tasks

17 Explain the importance of the Brezhnev Doctrine.

18 Explain why the USA did not openly support Czechoslovakia in 1968.

Activities

3 Look back at the Hungarian Rising on pages 90–93. Compare and contrast the rising in Hungary in 1956 with the Prague Spring of 1968.

a Copy and complete the table below.

	Similarities	Differences
Conditions in the two countries		
Reforms		
Soviet intervention		

b Which of the two risings do you think was the greater threat to the USSR? Explain your reasons.

Study tip

This section focuses on Cold War crises. The bullet-point question is likely to ask which of any two crises was the greater danger to peaceful co-existence, world peace, the USSR or the USA. The nuclear arms race and space race is essential for understanding the dangers of these crises in the world.

Practice questions

Study **Source A** and then answer all three questions that follow.

Source A   Letter from five Communist Party officials in Czechoslovakia,
sent to the Soviet leader Leonid Brezhnev in August 1968

> The Party leadership is no longer able to defend itself against attacks
> on socialism, and is unable to organise resistance against right wing
> forces. We are appealing to you, Soviet Communists, with a request
> for you to give support with all means at your disposal. Only with
> your help can the Czechoslovak Socialist Republic be saved from
> right wing revolution.

1   In 1957 the USSR launched the first satellite. In 1969 the USA landed the first
man on the moon.

Describe the main events of the space race from 1957 to 1969.   *(4 marks)*

2   **Source A** suggests a reason for the Soviet armed intervention in Czechoslovakia in
1968.

Do you agree that this was the main reason for the Soviet intervention?

Explain your answer by referring to the purpose of the source as well as using its
content and your knowledge.   *(6 marks)*

3   Which was the greater threat to world peace in the 1960s:
  • the U2 Crisis of 1960;
  • the Cuban Missile Crisis of 1962?

You must refer to **both** reasons when explaining your answer.   *(10 marks)*

6.1

Why did détente collapse in the 1970s and 1980s?

President Reagan and General Secretary Gorbachev at the Geneva Summit, 1988

The 1970s were the years of *détente* – an easing in the tension of the Cold War. By 1970 both superpowers had begun to realise the dangers of war in the nuclear age. They had accepted each other's sphere of influence. The arms race was proving to be expensive for both sides. This led to a series of talks resulting in the **SALT** I agreement of 1972 and the Helsinki Agreement of 1975. This was a return to the policy of peaceful co-existence first developed by Khrushchev in the 1950s. China became a member of the UN. The American President visited the USSR and China and the Soviet leader visited the USA. Talks on the reduction of arms, known as SALT II, continued and Presidents Carter and Brezhnev signed the SALT II agreement in 1979. Events in Afghanistan led to the collapse of this period of détente and eventually to the collapse of Communism in Eastern Europe.

War in Afghanistan

Background

The USSR had been giving aid to Afghanistan since the 1950s. It had improved the country by building roads and pipelines for oil. In 1973 the monarchy of Afghanistan had been overthrown. A further change of government in 1978 brought the Soviet-backed communist group to power supported by the military. The communist government started to introduce Soviet-style communist reforms, which were directly opposed to the culture and traditions of the people of Afghanistan: the people of the countryside were mostly Muslims and had strict religious views.

Objectives

In this chapter you will learn about:

why the Soviets went into Afghanistan and its effects on the USSR

the renewal of the Cold War under President Reagan

opposition to the USSR in Poland – Solidarity

Gorbachev and change in the USSR

the end of Soviet Communism in Eastern Europe

the fall of the Berlin Wall and the end of the Cold War.

Key terms

SALT: short for 'Strategic Arms Limitation Talks', this is an agreement that limited the number of ballistic missiles each side could have.

∞links

See peaceful co-existence on page 87.

Study tip

You will not be asked questions on détente in the 1970s, but this is background to the collapse of détente in the 1980s, which is part of the specification.

They did not agree with many of the new laws that were introduced, such as the way that land was being distributed and the new marriage laws.

The government of Afghanistan, which was being advised by the USSR, was becoming more and more unpopular with the people of Afghanistan. At the end of the 1970s, this opposition turned into open rebellion and a civil war broke out in Afghanistan. All opposition was dealt with severely by the Afghan government, using the army. In 1979 large numbers of the army began to desert. The opposition to the government was getting stronger. From early 1979, before the Soviet invasion, this opposition was being financed and supplied by the USA. This was because the USA tended to support all anti-communist movements.

The opposition to the communist government in Afghanistan was led by a Muslim group called the mujahidin, who objected to what they saw as an attack on their religion by the communist government. They believed they were fighting a *jihad* (holy war) and received funds from the USA and a wealthy Saudi, Osama bin Laden, who supported and financed many Islamic groups. This opposition forced the Afghan government to ask the USSR for help. Tanks and weapons were sent by the USSR and then, at Christmas 1979, around 80,000 Soviet troops entered Afghanistan.

B *The position of Afghanistan*

Timeline

From Afghanistan to the end of the USSR

Jun	**1979**	Soviet and American leaders sign SALT II
Dec	**1979**	USSR invades Afghanistan
Jan	**1980**	SALT II not confirmed by US Senate
Jul	**1980**	USA boycotts the Moscow Olympics
Sep	**1980**	Solidarity founded in Poland
Jan	**1981**	Ronald Reagan becomes President of the USA
Dec	**1981**	Martial Law declared in Poland
Jul	**1983**	Lech Walesa awarded the Nobel Peace Prize
Jul	**1984**	USSR boycotts the Los Angeles Olympics
Mar	**1985**	Gorbachev becomes leader of USSR
Feb	**1989**	Last Soviet troops leave Afghanistan
Nov	**1989**	Berlin Wall comes down – end of the Cold War
Dec	**1991**	USSR breaks up into independent republics

Tasks

1. What were the 'dangers of war in the nuclear age'?

2. Explain the expression 'sphere of influence'.

3. Summarise the main features of détente in the 1970s.

Why did the USSR invade Afghanistan?

- The immediate cause was the preservation of the communist government in Afghanistan, which had appealed to the USSR to provide troops to preserve its security and help it in the fight against the mujahidin. The apparent collapse of the Afghan army was of great concern to the Soviets, who were afraid of losing their influence in the area.

- In January 1979 a Muslim revolt had overthrown the pro-American ruler of Iran and set up a Muslim government, which could spread to Afghanistan. The USSR wanted to protect Afghanistan from this.

- There were 30 million Muslims in the USSR who could be encouraged to rebel if another Muslim state were set up in Afghanistan.

- The USSR wanted to expand its influence in Asia to balance that of the USA and China, who both supported Pakistan.

- Strategically, Afghanistan would bring the USSR closer to the Middle East and the Soviets could put pressure on the oil supply route from the Middle East to Europe and the USA.

- The USSR was afraid that President Amin of Afghanistan was becoming too friendly with the West and other countries: there was evidence that he had sought support from the USA, China and Pakistan. The USSR thought that since he had taken control, he was eliminating opponents within the party, many of whom were Soviet supporters.

- The Soviets later claimed that they wanted to fight against the secret involvement of the USA in Afghanistan. No one believed this at the time, but the USA had been sending help to the rebels for six months before the Soviet invasion.

The reaction of President Carter

The US President, Jimmy Carter, immediately condemned the Soviet invasion as an act of interference and a threat to world peace. Although Brezhnev insisted that the USSR had gone into Afghanistan to protect it and that it would withdraw as soon as the position had stabilised, Carter said that the Soviets would have to pay the consequences for their action. In January 1980 the General Council of the UN voted 104 to 18 in favour of a resolution condemning the invasion. Brezhnev dismissed this criticism and argued that the UN did not have the right to involve itself in the internal affairs of Afghanistan. Opposition to the invasion came not only from the USA but also from China and Islamic nations throughout the world.

American uncertainty

The Americans were uncertain of the aims of the USSR in the area and feared that it wanted to obtain access for its navy to the Arabian Sea. This could interfere with the oil route from the Middle East to the West. Carter sent a US force to the Arabian Sea to protect the oil routes, stating that the USA would resist any attempt by an opposing force to gain control of the Persian Gulf. This is sometimes referred to as the Carter Doctrine because of its similarity to the Truman Doctrine of 1947. Trade between the USA and USSR in certain goods such as

Activity

This activity could be completed as a discussion or group activity.

1　Look at the reasons for the Soviet invasion of Afghanistan. Discuss the importance of each one and then try to rank them in order, beginning with the most important and ending with the least important. Explain the reasons for your final order.

⚯ links

For the Truman Doctrine, see page 76.

grain and technology equipment was suspended and Carter advised the Senate not to **ratify** the SALT II agreement. The Americans led a boycott of the 1980 Moscow Olympics, which was supported by 60 other nations. The USA continued to give financial support to the mujahidin and was joined in this by Britain and China.

The USA was a little disappointed by the support it received from Europe. The British government did not ban its athletes from going to the Moscow Olympics, but allowed individuals to decide for themselves. Only a few opted out of the occasion. The British team members did not take part in the opening ceremony and, when they won medals, the Olympic flag was raised aloft instead of the Union flag and the Olympic anthem was played instead of 'God Save the Queen'. The American boycott assisted the British sprinters in the 100 metres as the Americans had dominated this event in the past. At Moscow in 1980, Allan Wells won Britain's first gold medal in this event for 56 years.

Events of the war

The Soviets quickly captured the airport at Kabul, the capital of Afghanistan. This enabled troops to be airlifted into Afghanistan. President Amin was assassinated and replaced by Babrak Karmal, who set up a new communist government controlled by the USSR. All this was before the end of 1979. The problem for the Soviets was that their invasion led to more open warfare and increased nationalist feeling in Afghanistan. The early fighting was in the open and the Soviet troops were able to occupy many towns, but the mujahidin remained in control of the countryside – almost 80 per cent of Afghanistan. Although the USSR had total control of the air and possessed superior weapons, the rebels managed to resist them.

Key terms

Ratify: to approve; to formally agree to.

Did you know ??????

Only 81 nations took part in the Moscow Olympics, the lowest number since 1956.

Tasks

4 Why did other foreign powers object to the Soviet invasion of Afghanistan?

5 How did they show their opposition and what effect did this opposition have?

6 Use Source **C** to explain why Soviet forces were successful at the beginning of the invasion.

C *Soviet control of Afghanistan, 1979–89*

The mujahidin

The key to the fighting in Afghanistan was the geography of the country and the nature of the mujahidin. Afghanistan is a mountainous, arid country and the mujahidin were fighting a holy war to protect their country and religion against a foreign invader and what they regarded as an **atheistic** culture. Their aim was to set up a Muslim state in Afghanistan. They used the geography of Afghanistan to fight a guerrilla war against the Soviet troops. The Soviets had received no training in how to combat this type of fighting. The mujahidin attacked Soviet supply routes quickly and then disappeared into the mountains. Opposition to the USSR was spread out throughout the whole of Afghanistan, so there was no real centre where the Soviets could attack. As the Americans had found out in Vietnam, it was difficult to eliminate this type of opposition as the mujahidin received support from most of the population, who often housed them. This led to the Soviets bombing villages and destroying homes, farms and families, which resulted in hardship and starvation. However, these tactics did not get rid of the opposition. Soviet troops launched nine offensives between 1980 and 1985, with little success.

D *USSR tanks ambushed by the mujahidin*

Reagan and the renewal of the Cold War

President Carter's response to the Soviet invasion of Afghanistan meant an end of SALT II and to the spirit of détente that had existed in the 1970s. The American-led boycott of the Moscow Olympics in 1980 was counteracted by a Soviet boycott of the 1984 Olympic Games, which were held in Los Angeles. The USSR claimed that it had concerns about the safety of its athletes in such a hostile environment as the USA. The boycott was supported by 14 East European communist states and was much less successful than the 1980 boycott.

When Ronald Reagan became President of the USA in 1981, there was a further deterioration in the relationship between the USSR and USA. This is sometimes called the Second Cold War or simply a renewal of the Cold War after the détente of the 1970s. Reagan had been a famous Hollywood actor and was known to hate Communism. His presidency got off to a good start when American hostages who had been detained in Iran were released. In March 1981 an attempt to assassinate him failed and his courage and humour in his recovery made him more popular.

Reagan had promised a hard-line approach to Communism and this was partly the reason for his election as President. He promised the American people 'peace through strength'. Reagan had a close ally in Margaret Thatcher, who had become Prime Minister of Britain in 1979. In a speech to the British parliament in June 1982, he condemned Communism as evil and followed this up in March 1983 with a speech in the USA, often known as the 'Evil Empire' speech. He referred to Communism and the USSR as the focus of evil in the modern world.

> ❝ What I am describing now is a plan and a hope for the long term – the march of freedom and democracy which will leave Communism on the ash tray of history as it has left other tyrannies which stifle the freedom and muzzle the self expression of the people. ❞

E Extract from Reagan's speech to the British parliament, June 1982

Reagan used arguments like this to gain extra funding from US Congress for the increased spending on arms that he was planning. He appears to have decided that the best way to defeat the USSR was to get so far ahead of them that they had to give in and end the Cold War. Some of the measures he took were designed to threaten the USSR; others were designed to protect the USA. These were as follows:

- Massive increase in military spending: $325 billion in 1980 to $456 billion in 1987.
- Re-started the development of the neutron bomb in 1981. This could kill armoured soldiers by radiation, but would not destroy the buildings and contaminate the land like other nuclear bombs.
- Invested funds in the building of two bombers: one a more traditional type and another called the 'stealth bomber', which could avoid a country's defences.

Did you know ??????

A total of 140 nations attended the Los Angeles Olympics, more than any previous Olympic Games.

Key profile

Ronald Reagan

1911	Born 6 February
1937	Begins career as an actor in Hollywood
1966	Elected Governor of California
1980	Elected President of USA by overwhelming majority
1981	Takes up office as President; shot in an assassination attempt
1983	Makes 'Evil Empire' speech; announces Strategic Defensive Initiative (SDI, or 'Star Wars')
1984	Re-elected with even bigger majority
1989	Leaves office
1994	Diagnosed with Alzheimer's disease
2004	Dies 5 June

- Speeded up the development of the Peacekeeper missiles, which were more accurate than those currently in production.
- Installed Cruise missiles in Europe in 1983. These would take 10 minutes to reach the USSR.
- Announced the Strategic Defense Initiative (SDI) in 1983. This was a defensive shield that used laser technology to intercept and destroy incoming missiles.
- Assisted the mujahidin in the fight in Afghanistan against the USSR by providing them with money and arms. Several American politicians saw Afghanistan as the Soviet Vietnam and were determined to do everything they could to make things difficult for the USSR there, probably in the hope of exhausting the Soviet economy.

These policies of Reagan greatly concerned the USSR. In particular, the development of SDI, usually known as 'Star Wars' after the popular film of the time, could mean the end of Mutually Assured Destruction (MAD). This upset the balance of forces between the two superpowers and made the USSR feel more vulnerable.

Did you know ??????

Osama bin Laden was one of the anti-Soviet guerrillas funded by the USA in Afghanistan in the 1980s.

∞links

See page 95 for Mutually Assured Destruction (MAD).

Tasks

9   Why do you think the time when Reagan became President is referred to as the renewal of the Cold War?

10   What were the main features of this renewed Cold War?

11   Why do you think Reagan made the speech in Source **E** in Britain?

12   Explain why the USSR feared Reagan's policies.

13   Use Reagan's key profile to find evidence of the popularity of these policies in the USA.

14   Why do you think the USSR boycotted the Los Angeles Olympics in 1984?

15   Was this boycott successful? Compare it with the American-led boycott of the Moscow Olympics in 1980 to explain your answer.

Activity

This activity could be completed as a discussion or group activity.

2   The Americans blamed the Soviets for the failure of détente; the Soviets blamed the Americans. Summarise the evidence that the Americans and the Soviets would use to support their views. What conclusion does the evidence lead you to make? Who was more responsible for the failure of détente?

Solidarity in Poland

The formation of the first independent trade union in Poland, Solidarity, has its roots in the poor standard of life of people in Poland in the 1970s. In 1970 a series of price increases led to strikes and marches that resulted in the deaths of ordinary workers. Further price rises and shortages of basic food such as bread caused more disaffection with the communist government in 1976. In 1978 Pope John Paul II, a Polish Cardinal, was elected Pope. A year later, he visited Poland. Communist governments normally try to get rid of Christianity but this proved to be difficult in Poland because of the strength of the Roman Catholic faith there. Most of the people in Poland are Roman Catholics and the support of the Pope and Church for Solidarity encouraged them to challenge the communist government in an attempt to raise the standard of living of the people. The Polish population was becoming more aware that their standard of life was a long way behind that of workers in the West.

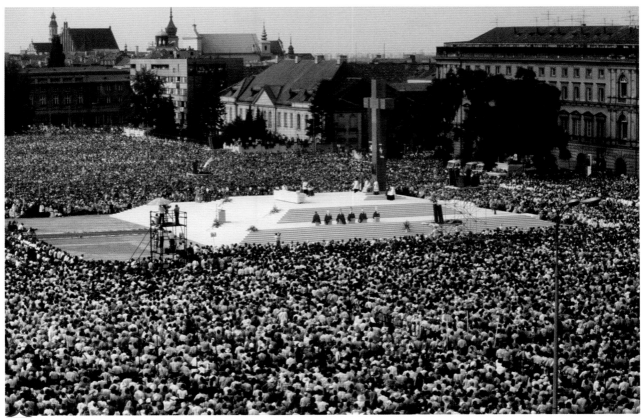

F *Pope John Paul II's first visit to Poland, 1979*

Opposition showed itself in the Gdansk shipyard in 1980. Two popular workers – one of whom was Lech Walesa, an outspoken electrician – had been dismissed by the authorities. Then the government raised the price of meat and allowed no wage increases. The workers in Gdansk refused to work and locked themselves into the shipyard in protest. Lech Walesa became their leader and they put forward 21 demands including the right to form independent trade unions, the end of censorship, more freedom for the Church and improvements in the national health system.

In spite of censorship, news of the strike spread throughout Poland. Strikes in other ports led to the shutdown of factories. In the Gdansk Agreement, the government agreed to accept the 21 demands. Solidarity, under the leadership of Lech Walesa, was recognised by the Polish government. Its membership totalled over 9 million in 1981. People joined Solidarity because they trusted it to improve their lives in general. At first, working conditions improved and Solidarity's popularity increased, not only in Poland but also in the West. Lech Walesa was seen as a folk hero in Poland and became an international figure. However, divisions began to surface within the trade union.

G *Lech Walesa addresses the strikers, 1980*

Walesa had always been careful not to challenge the authority of the USSR. He saw Solidarity as an organisation to improve working and living conditions for its members, not a political movement. He preferred negotiation with the government. In 1981 there were food shortages in Poland. Groups within Solidarity thought that Walesa was not going far enough and the USSR began to fear that Solidarity was beginning to act as a political party. The USSR was involved in Afghanistan and realised the popularity of Solidarity and Walesa in Europe. However, in December 1981 Soviet troops began to gather on the Polish border. This forced the Polish government to take action to prevent the break-up of Poland and a gap appearing in the Warsaw Pact.

The new Polish leader, General Jaruzelski, declared **martial law** in Poland. Overnight 5,000 members of Solidarity were arrested, including Walesa. Strikes were dealt with by the riot police, sometimes resulting in deaths. More arrests followed. In 1982 Solidarity was declared illegal. It continued as an underground movement with its own secret radio station and publications supported by the West, which kept its ideas alive. Walesa was released in November 1982 and martial law was lifted in July 1983, but food rationing remained. To show its support of Solidarity and its opposition to the Polish government, the West placed trade sanctions on Poland in 1983. This made the economic situation worse in the country.

Unrest continued and members of Solidarity were victimised when they were released from prison. In 1984 the secret police abducted and murdered Father Jerzy Popieluszko, a Catholic priest who was popular with the people. Lech Walesa's status as a world figure increased in July 1983 when he received the Nobel Peace Prize, but he was not allowed to leave the country to receive it in person.

Tasks

16 How do Sources **F** and **G** help you to understand events in Poland in the years 1979 to 1980?

17 Why did Solidarity have so much support in Poland in 1981?

18 How important was Lech Walesa in the opposition to the USSR from 1980 to 1983?

19 What had Walesa and Solidarity achieved in Poland by 1983?

20 Why do you think they had not achieved more?

Key terms

Martial law: government by the army involving the suspension of normal laws.

6.2   Why did Communism collapse in Central and Eastern Europe?

Mikhail Gorbachev

In the early 1980s the leaders of the USSR suffered from ill health. Brezhnev was ill for some time before his death in 1982. He was succeeded by Andropov, who ruled until his death in 1984, and Chernenko, who died in 1985. Both these leaders had recognised the talent of Mikhail Gorbachev and advanced his political career. Many had expected him to succeed Andropov but he was overlooked. However, his opportunity to improve the Soviet Union came in 1985. Although he was the youngest member of the *Politburo*, Gorbachev succeeded Chernenko as General Secretary of the Communist Party and therefore leader of the USSR. He became the first leader of the communist USSR to have been born after the Bolshevik Revolution of 1917. Gorbachev had a reputation for opposing corruption and was more open to reform than previous Soviet leaders, but the problems facing him were many.

By 1985 the USSR was involved in a costly war with Afghanistan and the economy was stagnating. Trade and industry were still organised as in the days of Stalin before the Second World War and, as a result, output was falling and the quality of goods was poor, particularly consumer goods as they often broke down. The communist system guaranteed everyone a home and a job and the people of the USSR were becoming slipshod in their approach to work. In earlier days, they had worked hard through fear of, or devotion to, the state. By the 1980s, the fear factor no longer existed and the workers were losing faith in the state. This meant that they had no incentive to work hard. The USSR could not keep up with the West in the new technological industries.

Many people in the USSR would have liked to have seen change, but the strict control of the Communist Party prevented this. As a result, people began to lose faith in the government, which was often seen as corrupt and lacking in ideas. The workforce had become disillusioned and depressed and many resorted to drink. Alcoholism became a major problem and this led to absenteeism from work and growing crime, contributing to the decline of the economy. At the same time, the USSR was involved in a costly arms race with the USA – a cost it could not afford. Gorbachev realised that reform was needed urgently if the USSR was to remain a force in the world. At the same time, although he realised that the need for reform was urgent, he also realised that he would have to move cautiously in case he upset party members who were loyal to Stalin's idea of Communism and did not want to see any changes.

Glasnost and *perestroika*

Gorbachev first tried to tackle the problem of alcoholism in the USSR. The price of alcoholic drinks, especially spirits, was raised, drinking in public places was forbidden and scenes of drinking were cut from films. His reforms did little to reduce the problem. Further upset came with the Chernobyl disaster of 1986, which appeared to show the weaknesses of Soviet industry to the world. It resulted in radioactive

> **Key terms**
>
> **Politburo:** the main policy-making committee of the Communist Party in the USSR.

> **Key profile**
>
> **Mikhail Gorbachev**
>
> | | |
> |---|---|
> | 1931 | Born 2 March in Stavropol, a rural region of the USSR |
> | 1952 | Joins the Communist Party |
> | 1954 | Graduates in law at Moscow University |
> | 1955 | Marries Raisa Titarenko |
> | 1970 | Becomes leader of the Communist Party in Stavropol |
> | 1978 | Put in charge of agriculture |
> | 1980 | Joins Politburo – the youngest full member |
> | 1985 | Appointed General Secretary of the Communist Party – the leader of the USSR |
> | 1990 | Awarded the Nobel Peace Prize |
> | 1991 | Resigns from office |
> | 1996 | Gains only 1 per cent of the vote when he was a candidate in the presidential election |

fallout that contaminated widespread areas. Many blamed Gorbachev for it, but in fact it proved the need for reform.

His main policies were those to reform the Soviet economy, introduced in 1986. These were originally known as the 'policy of acceleration' but became better known as *glasnost* and *perestroika*. Glasnost means 'openness' or 'opening up'; perestroika means 'restructuring' or 'reform'. They included policies that were similar to Dubcek's 'Communism with a human face', which had been suppressed in Czechoslovakia by the Soviet army in 1968.

Gorbachev described perestroika as a means of overcoming the process of stagnation by accelerating the economic progress of the USSR. It was not an attempt by Gorbachev to end Communism; it was an attempt to get rid of the inefficiency of the Soviet economy. Perestroika involved the introduction of private profit and competition in industry. With these incentives, he hoped that the Soviet economy would quickly recover. Many private cooperatives were set up and some of the huge state industries were split up into several private companies, which were all encouraged to acquire foreign investment to strengthen them.

Glasnost is the name given to Gorbachev's method of trying to eliminate corruption in government. It included an increase in free speech and a reduction in censorship. Criticism of the government was allowed and opponents of the government were permitted to return and resume their opposition in the open. Those who returned included the scientist Sakharov, who had been exiled from Moscow in 1980. Non-communists were allowed to stand for election. Gorbachev was trying to encourage open debate and make the people feel that they had a share in making the decisions and in this way help to restore their faith in the government. This freedom of information led to many of the brutalities of previous leaders being made known and the Soviet people were made more aware of the reality of their past.

> ❝ I want to put an end to all rumours in the West, and point out once again that all our reforms are socialist. We are looking within **socialism**, rather than outside it, for the answers to the questions that arise. Those who hope that we will move away from the socialist path will be greatly disappointed. ❞

A Extract from a speech by Gorbachev, 1987

Did you know ??????

When Gorbachev was asked what the difference was between his reforms and the Prague Spring, he is reported to have answered 'Eighteen years.'

∞ **links**

See Dubcek and Czechoslovakia on pages 110–112.

Did you know ??????

In 1988 school history exams were cancelled in the USSR because the textbooks were out of date after Gorbachev's policies of freedom of information.

Key terms

Socialism: Gorbachev was referring to Communism when he used this word.

Tasks

1. What were the main problems facing Gorbachev when he came to power in the USSR in 1985?

2. Explain how he tried to solve them.

3. What was new about his policies?

4. Read Source **A**.
   a. Explain the meaning of this source.
   b. Why do you think Gorbachev made this speech in 1987?

Gorbachev and Reagan

Gorbachev realised that the USSR could not keep up with the number of weapons being built by the USA and the cost of these weapons was a drain on the Soviet economy. Therefore, he announced that he would reduce Soviet spending on arms. It appeared to the Americans that here was a Soviet leader with a difference: one with whom they felt it would be possible to reach an agreement. Encouraged by Margaret Thatcher, who had met Gorbachev and claimed 'I like Mr Gorbachev, we can do business together', Reagan began to realise that Gorbachev was trying to change Soviet attitudes to the Cold War and started to change his own views. When he first met Gorbachev in Geneva in 1985, Reagan did not attack the 'Evil Empire'. Instead, he tried to convince Gorbachev that it was in the interests of both countries to negotiate and reach agreements.

This first meeting was followed by others, which eventually produced a reduction in nuclear arms. Reagan met Gorbachev in Iceland in 1986, and in 1987 Gorbachev was given a warm reception by the American public when he visited the USA. On that visit, the two powers signed the Intermediate Nuclear Forces (INF) Treaty, in which all medium-range nuclear missiles were banned, and Reagan agreed to stop work on the 'Star Wars' project. The treaty was confirmed in 1988 when Reagan visited Moscow.

Gorbachev and the war in Afghanistan

The war in Afghanistan which Gorbachev had inherited was another drain on the finances of the USSR. He realised that if his economic reforms were to succeed, he needed to reduce spending on arms and on the war in Afghanistan. The communist government set up by the Soviets in Afghanistan was unable to gain the trust of the people and there appeared to be no hope of victory. The Soviet army was affected by disease and unable to cope with the guerrilla tactics of the mujahidin. The war remained unpopular abroad and Gorbachev wanted to give a better image of the USSR to the USA in particular.

Soviet tactics in Afghanistan

Soviet tactics in Afghanistan changed in 1986. They became far more defensive and there were few major offensives. The USSR concentrated mostly on using the air, but the USA supplied the mujahidin with anti-aircraft weapons from 1987 and these led to further Soviet losses of lives and equipment. Gorbachev announced that he was beginning the withdrawal of troops in 1986, but the first withdrawals were replaced. It was not until February 1988 that he announced the full withdrawal of the USSR from Afghanistan. This was completed in 1989.

Did you know ??????

Ronald Reagan at 77 is the oldest American President to have held office.

⊂⊃ links

See pages 116–120 for more on Afghanistan.

B *Soviet troops withdrawing from Afghanistan*

The effects of war in Afghanistan

- Around 15,000 Soviet troops were killed, with over half a million casualties.
- The USSR lost much heavy equipment including planes, tanks and armoured vehicles.
- The enormous expense crippled the Soviet economy.
- The war proved that the Red Army was not invincible, so it could no longer be relied on to keep the Soviet Empire together. Questions would be asked in the USSR regarding the huge cost of maintaining an armed force that could not defeat the Afghans.
- The effect on army and economy contributed to the collapse of the Soviet Empire in Eastern Europe.
- Over 1 million Afghans died, including children killed by Soviet mines. This increased the Afghans' hatred of foreigners.
- The Soviet withdrawal did not end the war: the civil war continued until 1992 when the Mujahidin captured Kabul from the communist government.
- Afghanistan became a centre for terrorist activity.

Tasks

5   Look back at Reagan and the renewal of the Cold War on pages 121–122. Why do you think President Reagan changed his attitude to Communism in 1985?

6   Explain the main reasons for the Soviet withdrawal from Afghanistan.

7   Why do you think the USSR failed to defeat the mujahidin?

8   Explain how the war in Afghanistan weakened the USSR.

Hint

Refer back to pages 116–120 to help with your answers to Tasks 7 and 8.

Gorbachev and Eastern Europe

The situation in Eastern Europe was similar to that in the USSR. Poor living standards and shortages of food led to criticism of the communist leaders. Gorbachev's changes in the USSR brought more demands from the people in the satellite states. They wanted glasnost and perestroika to exist in their countries, and so did Gorbachev. The problem was the communist rulers of the states of Eastern Europe. Most of them were old and steeped in the doctrines of Communism. They were afraid of change and uncertain that Gorbachev's reforms would work. They feared that reforms like glasnost and perestroika might lead to popular risings, which could threaten the government and their position of authority.

Gorbachev realised that the Soviet economy could no longer support the governments of Eastern Europe. Moreover, a relaxation of control over Eastern Europe would help his aim to improve relations with the USA. It would also make the USSR more attractive to foreign investment, which Gorbachev realised was needed to bring about economic recovery. In 1988 he abandoned the Brezhnev Doctrine and in 1989 the leaders of the communist states in Eastern Europe were informed that they could no longer rely on the Red Army to support them. This meant that there could be no repeat of what had happened in Hungary in 1956 and Czechoslovakia in 1968. The rulers of Eastern Europe would have to relax their rule and listen to the demands of their people. This led to great changes.

Timeline

The collapse of Communism in Eastern Europe

Dec	**1988**	Gorbachev abandons the Brezhnev Doctrine
Jun	**1989**	Solidarity wins seats in Polish elections
Jul	**1989**	Gorbachev warns that the Red Army would not support other communist rulers
Aug	**1989**	Hungary opens its border with the West
Oct	**1989**	Other political parties are allowed in Hungary
Nov	**1989**	The borders of East Germany are opened – end of the Berlin Wall
Dec	**1989**	Summit Meeting in Malta – end of Cold War; Havel elected President of Czechoslovakia
Oct	**1990**	West and East Germany reunited
Dec	**1990**	Lech Walesa becomes President of Poland
Jun	**1991**	Boris Yeltsin elected President of Russia
Jul	**1991**	Warsaw Pact ends
Aug	**1991**	Coup against Gorbachev in USSR
Dec	**1991**	Gorbachev resigns – end of the USSR; Yeltsin becomes President of the Russian Federation

∞ links

See pages 90–93 for the Hungarian Rising and pages 110–113 for Czechoslovakia and the Brezhnev Doctrine.

The end of Soviet control in Eastern Europe

Poland

Although Solidarity had been illegal since 1981, it continued to oppose Jaruzelski's communist government throughout the 1980s. Lech Walesa remained an international figure and organised strikes for better working conditions. Influenced by Gorbachev's reforms in the USSR and under pressure from strikes, the Polish government entered talks with Walesa in September 1988. This resulted in partially free elections. Walesa's party won all the seats that were open to them. Even though the communists were guaranteed victory in many seats as no other party was allowed to stand for election in them, they failed to win a majority. Jaruzelski tried to persuade Walesa to form a coalition with the communists, but Walesa refused. At the end of 1989 the first non-communist government in the former Soviet satellite states was set up in Poland, although the country was still communist in name. In December 1990 Jaruzelski resigned and Lech Walesa became President of Poland.

C *Riot police at work in Poland, 1982*

D *Lech Walesa in talks in Warsaw, 1989*

Tasks

9   Describe what is happening in Sources **C** and **D**.

10   What type of people do you think the riot police were attacking in Source **C**?

11   What was Lech Walesa doing in 1982?

12   What do you think was the main reason for the change in Walesa's position between 1982 and 1989?

Hungary

The changes in Hungary were achieved more smoothly than in other countries of Eastern Europe. From 1956 to 1988, Hungary had been ruled by Kadar, until he was forced to resign through ill health which led to his death in 1989. Kadar had gained some measure of independence for Hungary from the USSR. He carried out reforms to the economy in Hungary and they began trading with the West. However, Kadar remained a loyal supporter of the Warsaw Pact: the Hungarian army took part in putting down the Prague Spring in Czechoslovakia in 1968. Kadar's successors allowed a peaceful change from Communism to democracy in Hungary.

The reformers in the Communist Party were admitted to the government after Kadar's resignation and measures similar to Glasnost were introduced in Hungary. The rising of 1956 began to be referred to as a 'popular uprising' and in June 1989 Nagy's body, which had been buried in an unmarked grave in 1956, was given a public reburial in Budapest. Between 50,000 and 100,000 attended the re-burial. The first break in the Iron Curtain occurred in August when Hungary opened its border with democratic Austria. In October, the Communist Party allowed other parties to stand for election and in 1990 the Hungarian Republic was declared and free parliamentary elections held. The last Soviet troops left Hungary in 1991.

⊙⊙ links

Turn back to pages 90–93 for more on the Hungarian Rising.

Tasks

13 Look back at Source **E** on page 93. What was the importance of calling this rising a 'popular uprising' in 1989?

14 What was the importance of the reburial of Nagy in 1989?

15 Why do you think the changes in Hungary in 1989 were achieved more smoothly than in other Eastern European countries?

E *Hungarians take down a red star, the symbolism of Communism, March 1990*

Czechoslovakia

After the Prague Spring of 1968, Czechoslovakia was ruled by Husak. His rule was less harsh than that of many other Eastern European rulers and Czechoslovakia underwent some reform, but the hated secret police still existed and threatened the freedom of the people. Many of the opponents of Communism emigrated to the West and opposition within the country was limited to small groups. In March 1987 the communist government of Czechoslovakia announced that it was committed to reforms similar to those of Gorbachev in the USSR. Although stating publicly that he supported the changes, Husak was not fully committed to glasnost and perestroika. Progress with these reforms was slow, which led to a series of demonstrations in the main cities of Prague and Bratislava in 1988 and 1989. In November 1989 the police used violence to break up a demonstration in favour of democracy.

⚮links

See Dubcek and the Prague Spring on pages 110–113.

Activities

1. Why do you think the changes in Czechoslovakia in 1989 were called the Velvet Revolution?

2. Why was Dubcek popular with the reformers in 1989?

F *Crowds in Wenceslas Square in Prague, Czechoslovakia, protesting against the communist government, November 1989*

The demand for reform and the violence of the police led to the formation of a group campaigning for change, led by Havel. Havel was a writer who had criticised the government since the Prague Spring of 1968. Under the communists, he had served multiple sentences in prison for his opposition, the longest being a sentence of about four years. In 1989, Havel was supported by Dubcek, the leader responsible for the Prague Spring reforms in 1968. The unpopularity of the government and the demands of the USSR for reform resulted in a speedy collapse of the communists in Czechoslovakia in what was known as the Velvet Revolution. Faced with growing opposition, Husak resigned and Havel was elected President on 29 December 1989. Dubcek became Chairman ('Speaker') of the Parliament. Free elections were held in 1990, resulting in a massive victory for the parties supporting democracy.

East Germany

The leader of East Germany, Honecker, refused to put Gorbachev's reforms into effect in East Germany. Thousands of East Germans took advantage of Hungary opening its border with the West and fled to the West through Hungary. Others showed their opposition by a series of demonstrations and protest marches. Gorbachev visited the country and urged the communist government to carry out reforms, but Honecker refused. On 18 October Honecker was forced to step down as leader and was replaced by Krenz. This was an attempt by the government to get rid of the opposition, but it failed. Rallies in favour of democracy were held and East Germans continued to move to West Germany through Hungary and Czechoslovakia. The communist government resigned on 7 November and on 9 November the border with West Germany was opened. In Berlin, crowds marched to the Berlin Wall and began pulling it down. The Brandenburg Gate was opened on 22 December and free elections were held in East Germany on 18 March 1990. The old East Germany collapsed and on 3 October 1990 East and West Germany were once again united.

"I haven't demolished the Berlin Wall, but I've jolly well demolished the NATO one!"

H *A British cartoon on the Berlin Wall, 1989*

Did you know ??????

Most West Germans welcomed the reunification of Germany, but there were some who feared the effect that the number of people moving from east to west might have on the economy of the new Germany.

G *The fall of the Berlin Wall, November 1989*

Task

16 What do Sources **E**, **F** and **G** tell you about popular views in Eastern Europe in 1989–90?

17 Compare the ways in which Poland, Hungary, Czechoslovakia and East Germany obtained democracy.

a How were these ways similar and how were they different?

b Which country do you think had the smoothest change and in which country were the changes the most difficult? Give reasons for these differences.

18 Explain the meaning of Source **H**. Do you think it is an accurate view of what Gorbachev had achieved?

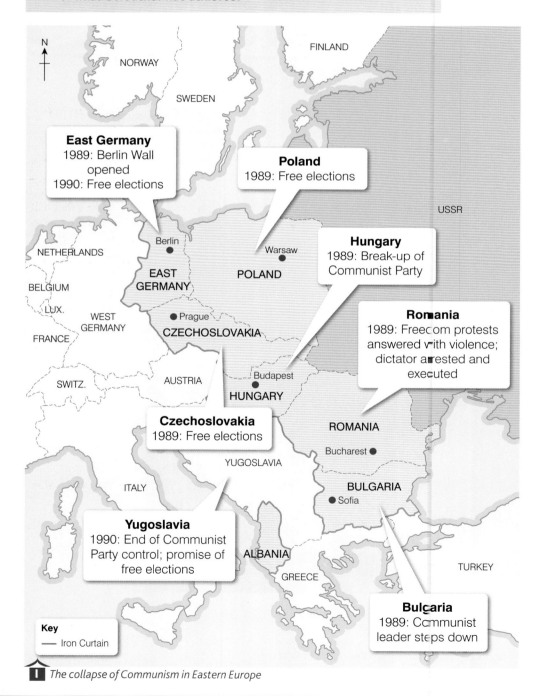

East Germany
1989: Berlin Wall opened
1990: Free elections

Poland
1989: Free elections

Hungary
1989: Break-up of Communist Party

Romania
1989: Freedom protests answered with violence; dictator arrested and executed

Czechoslovakia
1989: Free elections

Yugoslavia
1990: End of Communist Party control; promise of free elections

Bulgaria
1989: Communist leader steps down

Key
— Iron Curtain

I The collapse of Communism in Eastern Europe

The end of the Cold War

The beginning of the end of the Cold War was at the Summit Meeting in Reykjavik, Iceland, in 1986 when President Gorbachev proposed enormous reductions in the number of nuclear weapons held by the USA and the USSR. Although this approach failed, the move to disarmament was confirmed in the Washington Treaty signed at the end of 1987.

Gorbachev's reforms in the USSR and the movement to increased democracy in Eastern Europe did much to further improve relations between the USA and the USSR. The collapse of the Berlin Wall meant the end of the Iron Curtain. Shortly after this, the leaders of the two superpowers met at a Summit Meeting held in Malta at the beginning of December 1989. It was the first Summit Meeting for the new American President, George H. W. Bush, who had been Reagan's Vice President and then replaced him as President in 1989. Although no agreements were actually signed at the Summit, after the meeting Gorbachev and Bush made statements that are often regarded as the end of the Cold War.

links
See page 127 to recap on Gorbachev and Reagan.

links
For more information on the Iron Curtain, see pages 74–75.

Did you know ???????

George H. W. Bush was President of the USA from 1989 to 1993. His eldest son is George W. Bush, who was President of the USA from 2001 to 2009.

> " The world is leaving one epoch and entering another. We are at the beginning of a long road to a lasting, peaceful era. The threat of force, mistrust, psychological and ideological struggle should all be things of the past. I assured the President of the United States that I will never start a hot war against the USA. "

J Gorbachev speaking at the news conference held after the Malta Summit

> " We can realise a lasting peace and transform the East–West relationship to one of enduring cooperation. That is the future that Chairman Gorbachev and I began right here in Malta. "

K George Bush responding to Gorbachev at the news conference held after the Malta Summit

> " Ronald Reagan had a higher claim than any other leader to have won the Cold War for liberty and he did it without a shot being fired. "

L Margaret Thatcher on Ronald Reagan, after his death in 2004

> " I think we all lost the Cold War, particularly the Soviet Union. We each lost $10 trillion ... we only won when the Cold War ended. "

M Gorbachev reflects on the Cold War, 2004

> " Mr Gorbachev deserves most of the credit as leader of this country. "

N Reagan speaking in 1988 at a press conference in Moscow on the reasons for the end of the Cold War

The collapse of the USSR

Gorbachev has been praised in the West for the part he played in ending the Cold War and reforming the USSR. However, he was less popular in the USSR. Although his new policies were greeted enthusiastically, his popularity was soon reduced. His economic policies failed because the old structures of the USSR acted against them. Food shortages remained, resulting in rationing of some goods. Gorbachev probably thought that Communism would be reformed by his policies; he did not expect it to collapse. Many communists considered that Gorbachev had betrayed the movement and saw the end of Soviet influence in Eastern Europe as a disaster. Others who supported the reforms, such as Boris Yeltsin, who had been promoted within the party by Gorbachev, thought that Gorbachev was moving too slowly. They wanted more political democracy and more power passed to the separate republics that made up the USSR.

Gorbachev's own views on reform added to his problems. His policy of glasnost meant that the criticism became public. The removal of censorship led to the media commenting on the weaknesses of the Soviet economy. For over half a century, the Soviet people had only been given positive news by the media; now the removal of communist control of the media meant that they were receiving negative reports. They began to lose all faith and trust in their political system. The movement to greater independence in Eastern Europe also affected the individual states of the USSR, which began to demand more freedom and independence from the USSR. Gorbachev was faced with demonstrations all over the USSR from people who wanted further reform and independence.

Hint

In Task 19, test Source **L** using your knowledge, then look at the provenance of the source and explain if it could lead to exaggeration.

Tasks

19 Do you agree that the reason given in Source **L** was the main reason for the end of the Cold War? Explain your answer.

20 Explain the meaning of Source **M**. How accurate do you think it is? Give reasons for your answer.

21 Do you think Source **N** is more or less accurate than Source **L**? Explain your answer.

22 Why do you think Gorbachev was awarded the Nobel Peace Prize in 1990?

O *Boris Yeltsin addresses the crowd during the Coup of August 1991*

Yeltsin becomes President of the Russian Federation

Yeltsin had been dismissed from the Politburo by Gorbachev, but in 1990 he was elected Chairman of the Russian Parliament. In June 1991 Yeltsin was elected President of the Russian Republic, defeating Gorbachev's preferred candidate. In August 1991 extreme communists opposed to Gorbachev rebelled against him and tried to seize power. Gorbachev was placed under house arrest, but Yeltsin rallied the people and stood up to the rebels. Yeltsin's action caused the coup to collapse. Gorbachev returned to power, but his position was weakened.

With demands for independence coming from its member states, including Ukraine which voted for independence from the USSR in December 1991, the USSR was collapsing. On 25 December 1991, Gorbachev resigned and the USSR was formally dissolved the next day. Boris Yeltsin became the President of the Russian Federation, which replaced the USSR in the UN.

Activities

These activities could be completed as a discussion, debate, group work, role-play or simply to plan an argument from different points of view.

3   Read the following reasons for the collapse of Communism in Eastern Europe.

a   The war in Afghanistan weakened the USSR.

b   President Reagan's policies of challenging the USSR led to the USSR spending too much on arms and not enough on its people.

c   Opposition to Communism, particularly the Solidarity movement in Poland, weakened it.

d   Gorbachev's policies brought opposition into the open and meant that Communism was bound to collapse.

4   Get as much evidence as you can to support and oppose each of the above reasons.

5   Using the evidence you have obtained, make a list of the reasons, putting the one you feel was most important at the top of the list, followed by the next and so on, until at the bottom is the reason that you consider was the least important.

6   Explain why you have listed the reasons in this order.

Tasks

23   Why do you think Gorbachev was unpopular in the USSR in 1991 but popular in the West?

24   Study Source **O**.

a   What impression does this source give of Boris Yeltsin?

b   Do you think the coup weakened or increased his popularity in the USSR?

25   Explain the part played by Yeltsin in the division of the USSR.

26   Who do you think played the greater part in this, Yeltsin or Gorbachev? Give reasons for your answer.

Study tip

The stem of the bullet-point question is likely to centre on the two key questions in this chapter and you will be asked to assess the contribution of any two points to the answering of the key question.

Practice questions

Study **Source A** and then answer the questions that follow.

Source A From *Tearing Down the Curtain: The People's Revolution in Eastern Europe* by J. Flint and N. Hawkes, 1990

> Communist power in Eastern Europe has collapsed like a house cf cards. Regimes that stood unchanged for 40 years have been swept away in a few weeks of revolutionary activity by the people taking to the streets.

1 In 1985 Mikhail Gorbachev came to power in the USSR and intoduced a number of reforms.

   Describe Gorbachev's policies of perestroika and glasnost.   *(4 marks)*

2 **Source A** suggests a reason for the end of communist control in Eastern Europe by 1990.

   Do you agree that this was the main reason for the collapse?

   Explain your answer by referring to the purpose of the source as well as using its content and your knowledge.   *(6 marks)*

3 Which was more important for the collapse of détente in the 1980s:
   • the Soviet invasion of Afghanistan;
   • the policies of US President Ronald Reagan?

   You must refer to **both** reasons when explaining your answer.   *(10 marks)*

Glossary

A

Alliance: an agreement between two or more countries to support each other.

Annex: to join or unite; to take possession of.

Atheistic: a way of life that does not believe in the existence of god.

Autocratic: having complete power.

B

Brinkmanship: a policy of risking war to achieve your aims – pushing the other power to the edge.

C

CIA: Short for 'Central Intelligence Agency', this is the American civilian body that collects information about foreign governments to aid American decision-making.

Collective security: if one state attacked another, all the members would join together and act against the aggressor.

Conscription: conscription means compulsory enrollment in the military for a definite or indefinite period of service. Many countries nowadays make conscription compulsory for young men and women for a definite period, usually 1 or 2 years.

D

Dardanelles: part of the strategic waterway linking the Mediterranean to the Black Sea.

Diktat (of Versailles): 'dictated peace' – the Germans called the treaty this because Germany was forced to sign it.

Domino Effect: the belief that if one country became communist, those next to it would fall to Communism like a pack of dominoes.

E

Espionage: spying – the use of secret agents to collect information, normally of a military nature.

G

Guernica: an undefended town in Spain which was bombed for three hours by the Germans in 1937, resulting in 2,500 casualties.

I

Ideology: a set of beliefs and characteristics.

M

Mandate: the power to rule a country granted by the League in preparation for self-government.

Martial law: government by the army involving the suspension of normal laws.

Mobilise: to get troops ready for war.

N

Neutral: a country that favours neither side in a dispute or war.

P

Pact: an agreement between countries.

Patriots: people who are prepared to defend the rights and freedoms of their own country.

Plebiscite: a vote by the people on a question of national importance.

Politburo: the main policy-making committee of the Communist Party in the USSR.

Q

Quarantine: a period of isolation.

R

Ratify: to approve; to formally agree to.

Reparations: compensation to be paid by the defeated powers to the victorious powers for the cost of the war.

Republic: a government chosen by the people with an elected president.

S

SALT: Short for 'Strategic Arms Limitation Talks', this is an agreement that limited the number of ballistic missiles each side could have.

Satellite state: a country that is independent, but under the heavy influence or control of another country.

Self-determination: the right of all people to decide which country they will be ruled by.

Subjugation: conquest.

T

Tsar: the emperor of Russia; also spelt czar.

U

U-boat: German name for a submarine, short for *Unterseebot (U-Boot)*.

Ultimatum: a final demand with a threat of force if you do not agree.

V

Veto: a vote that blocks a decision being put into effect.

W

War indemnity: a sum of money that a country is forced to pay if it is defeated in war.

Weltpolitik: meaning 'world policy', this phrase is often used to describe Kaiser Wilhelm's desire to be a major player in world affairs.

Index

Acknowledgements

The authors and publisher would like to thank the following for permission to reproduce material:

p61 short extract from Winston Churchill's speech at Fulton Missouri, 5 March 1946, reprinted with permission of Curtis Brown Ltd, London, on behalf of The Estate of Winston Churchill; p75 short extract from Winston Churchill's speech in Parliament, 5 October 1938, reprinted with permission of Curtis Brown Ltd, London, on behalf of The Estate of Winston Churchill; p95 short extract (table) from Gerards Segal, *The Simon & Schuster Guide to the World Today*, Simon & Schuster, 1987; p102 short extract from *GCSE Modern World History* 2/e by Ben Walsh, John Murray, 2001, reprinted with permission of John Murray Ltd.

Photographs courtesy of:

Ann Ronan Picture Library pp14, 68, 83, 90, 94, 94, 94, 96; Cartoon Museum University of Kent pp39, 60; Corbis pp10,11, 16, 50 (bottom), 54, 78 (top), 101, 102, 120, 123, 124, 132, Edimedia Art Archive pp18, 23, 27, 29, 50 (margin), 82, 85, 92, 97, 108, 116, 133; Getty p110; Mary Evans Picture Library pp35, 61; Photo12 pp6, 30, 46, 59, 62, Public Domain pp20, 36, 73, 73, 77; Topfoto pp41, 42, 67, 78 (bottom), 81, 88, 91, 106, 112, 128, 130, 130, 131, 133, 136; World History Archive pp9, 19, 25, 26, 48, 65, 71, 72, 80, 99.

Front cover photograph courtesy of Rex Features.

Photo Research by Alexander Goldberg, Dora Swick, Ann Asquith and Tara Roberts of Image Asset Management, 1556 Stratford Road, Birmingham, B28 9HA. Special thanks to James Clift and Jason Newman of Image Content Collections.

Every effort has been made to trace the copyright holders, but if any have been inadvertently overlooked the publishers will be pleased to make the necessary arrangements at the first opportunity.